Country Roads
~ of ~
GEORGIA

*A Guide Book
from Country Roads Press*

Country Roads
~ of ~
GEORGIA

Carol and Dan Thalimer

Illustrated by
Victoria Sheridan

Country Roads Press
CASTINE · MAINE

Country Roads of Georgia
© 1995 by Carol and Dan Thalimer. All rights reserved.

Published by Country Roads Press
P.O. Box 286, Lower Main Street
Castine, Maine 04421

Text and cover design by Edith Allard.
Illustrations by Victoria Sheridan.
Typesetting by Camden Type 'n Graphics.

ISBN 1-56626-124-4

Library of Congress Cataloging-in-Publication Data
Thalimer, Carol.
    Country Roads of Georgia / by Carol Thalimer with
    Dan Thalimer.
        p. cm.
    Includes index.
    ISBN 1-56626-124-4 : $9.95
    1. Georgia—Tours. 2. Automobile travel—Georgia—
    Guidebooks. I. Thalimer, Dan. II. Title.
    F384.3.T48   1995
    917.5804'43—dc20   94-45470
                                                            CIP

Printed in the United States of America.
10   9   8   7   6   5   4   3   2   1

To Karin Koser and crew

Captain of Police
Retired, Berkeley

Chief of Police
Retired, Alameda

RICHARD YOUNG
Law Enforcement Consultant

1119 Holly Street
Alameda, California 94501
415/521-1500

Post Office Box 15
Kyburz, CA 95720
916/293-3221

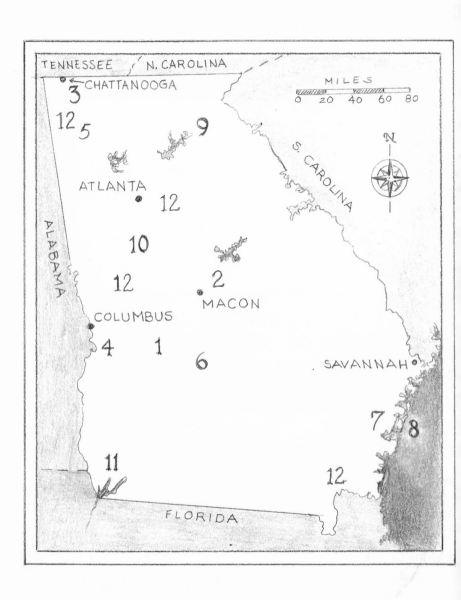

Contents

(& Key to Georgia Country Roads)

Acknowledgments

The Georgia Department of Industry, Trade and Tourism is an invaluable resource. Especially helpful were Karin Koser, Cheryl Smith, Dawn Townsend, Becky Basset, Kitty Sikes, Barbara Daniell, Mary Jo Dudley, Jeannie Buttram, Carol Spires, and Fay Tripp. A special thanks to Ellen and David Archer and Kenneth Holcomb for sharing their vast Northwest Georgia Civil War knowledge with us.

Introduction

We've lived in Georgia for fifteen years and loved every minute of it—with the possible exceptions of Snow Jam '82 and the Snowstorm of the Century in 1993.

We used to own several travel agencies and jetted around the world to exotic locations so we could advise our customers from firsthand experience. Although we knew that Georgia had much to offer the resident, we thought our adopted state had little to entice the tourist. We have to confess our guilt in telling people that "Georgia is a great place to live, but we wouldn't want to visit there." The trouble was we hadn't bothered to look.

When we became regular travel columnists for several Atlanta newspapers, we alternated articles about foreign destinations with those about more localized sites, so we had to do some research. When we actually looked beyond the ends of our noses, we were stunned with the surprises our adopted state offers—beaches, forests, mountains, waterfalls, lakes, canyons, swamps, and natural springs with therapeutic powers. Georgia has significant Native American, Spanish, English, French, and Civil War history.

In researching our *Georgia B&Bs* and *Georgia Outdoor Activity Guide* (both Country Roads Press, 1994), we visited every corner of Georgia. Now we proclaim, "Not only is Georgia a fabulous place to live, we love to visit there."

Despite the network of interstate highways, Georgia remains a largely rural state dotted with small villages connected by country roads. Large towns and even the metropolis of Atlanta are actually made up of a series of little hamlets or neighborhoods.

You'll find Georgia's small towns remarkably similar in appearance, although each is unique in character. After the devastation of the Civil War and Reconstruction, the state entered a golden age fueled by the railroads. Because of successful railroad expansion, scores of small towns arose along the routes during the last twenty years of the nineteenth century, when Victorian architecture was the predominant style.

Commercial buildings followed the Italianate fashion, whereas large homes were often Queen Anne or Second Empire in design. Much of this outstanding architecture has been preserved. Many turn-of-the-century mercantile buildings now serve as businesses, museums, and hotels; numerous houses have been reborn as restaurants, bed and breakfasts, and intimate inns.

Two other architectural legacies of that extravagant period are the magnificent county courthouses and the less excessive, but nonetheless picturesque, railroad depots. Georgia, largest state east of the Mississippi, has more counties than any other state in the union—159. It seems as if every town larger than a crossroads is a county seat and boasts a charming town square on which is centered an opulent courthouse. Many of the surviving depots serve as Chambers of Commerce, welcome centers, restaurants, boutiques, and museums. While exploring any of Georgia's trails, make a photographic collection of its courthouses and depots.

Georgia's many counties can be confusing to the out-of-state visitor. One peculiarity is that many towns are not in the county of the same name. For example, Lumpkin is not in Lumpkin County, and Clayton is not in Clayton County. But just when you think you're getting the hang of it, you'll come across Thomasville in Thomas County and Tifton in Tift County.

Although the economy of the state has prospered through one transportation system or another—first railway, then highway, and now airline—a primary source of income has always revolved around agriculture—first cotton, now peaches, pecans, peanuts, and sweet Vidalia onions. Farms and orchards provide interesting tours, as do food processing plants such as Claxton Fruitcakes and Stuckey's Candy.

In addition to the nine tourism regions created by the Georgia Department of Industry, Trade and Tourism, the state has designated several trails that are perfect for exploring the state by country roads. These trails, which focus on such diverse themes as Native American lore, Civil War history, and agriculture, are the Andersonville Trail, Civil War history, 75 miles; Antebellum Trail, architecture/Civil War history, 100 miles; Blue and Gray Trail, Civil War history, 150 miles; Chattahoochee Trace, waterways/history, 200 miles; Chieftans Trail, Native American history, 150 miles; Peach Blossom Trail, agriculture/history, 200 miles; as well as the Antiques Trail, central Georgia, 180 miles; Miracle in the Mountains Loop Tour, Northwest Georgia, 170 miles; Treasures Between the Trails, central Georgia, 90 miles; and Wiregrass/301 Trail, southeast Georgia, 175 miles.

In addition, we've devised several trails of our own: Classic Magnolias, history, 250 miles; Coastin' Along Georgia's Seaboard, early Georgia history, 100 miles; Golden Isles, beaches/history, 100 miles; Mountain Magic, scenery/ shopping, 250 miles; and Plantation Trace, antebellum history, 200 miles.

We'd suggest touring the Peach State by choosing one of the trails we describe. Whether it takes you a weekend or a week to explore the trail's sites depends on how thorough you are. When a town appears in more than one trail, we've described it in one write-up and made reference to it in the other.

We've concentrated on sight-seeing attractions, although we do mention lakes, rivers, hiking trails, and the like.

We do not include dates, times, or admission prices because they are so changeable. Some attractions with major architectural and/or historical significance are private homes that are not open to the public or are open just for special occasions, so you may only be able to walk or drive by. For the most current information on attractions, check with the local welcome center when you plan your trip or when you get to the area.

If you stop to ask directions when traveling around Georgia, don't be surprised if you get some blank stares. You've probably mispronounced something. For example, Albany is pronounced All BEN nie; Houston isn't pronounced as it is in Texas but as HOUSE-ton; LaFayette is La FAY ette, and Vienna is VIE enna.

Some of the accommodations and attractions we describe are in Georgia's state parks, most of which charge a small entrance fee. Look into a $25.00 Georgia ParkPass, which gives you unlimited access to the parks. The pass can be purchased at any park or historic site. For more information or a free color brochure, call 656-3530 in metro Atlanta or 1-800-3GA-PARK in the rest of Georgia.

To help clarify road designations, we've used the following abbreviations: I=interstate, US=US route or highway, and State=state route or highway.

Tracing Georgia's engaging trails will provide you with many enjoyable vacations. When you've explored all the ones described here, you still won't have covered all of Georgia, so be creative and make up your own trails.

1 ~

Andersonville Trail

Getting there: Exit I-75 onto State 127 West at Perry.

Highlights: *Civil War history, Boehm porcelain birds, Jimmy Carter's hometown, watermelon capital of the world, and the Big Pig Jig.*

Although the Andersonville Trail is named for the infamous Civil War prison camp where 13,000 Union soldiers died, the seventy-five-mile trail offers more than Civil War history as it meanders through West Georgia from Perry to Cordele, passing gardens, villages, outstanding architectural treasures, historic sites, and natural wonders. Spend a long weekend following the trail, staying a night or two in one of the many quaint bed and breakfasts along the way.

Exit I-75 onto State 127 west at Perry (see Peach Blossom Trail). After you've explored Perry, proceed west on State 127 to Marshallville, which is the National Headquarters of the

American Camellia Society. Massee Lane Gardens maintains gardens, a greenhouse, a research library, and an extensive collection of famous Boehm porcelain birds (see the Peach Blossom Trail).

From Marshallville, turn south on State 49. The highlight of the Andersonville Trail and the next stop is the Andersonville National Historic Site, a Civil War prison park and national cemetery, which tells the heart-wrenching story of Andersonville's place in history. Camp Sumter, as the fort was officially known in Civil War times, was the largest Confederate military prison. Confederate officials had decided they needed to move federal prisoners away from Richmond to a place of greater safety and more abundant food, so they picked Andersonville, deep in West Georgia. Although the stockade is gone, ridges mark the perimeter of the fort. Today the 475-acre site remains an active national cemetery and the country's only national memorial for prisoners of war throughout America's history.

The prison pen began as 16.5 acres enclosed by a fifteen-foot-high stockade, but it was later enlarged to 26.5 acres. Inside, nineteen feet from the barricade, was the "deadline," a boundary that prisoners were forbidden to cross on threat of death. Although the prison was built to handle 10,000 prisoners at a time, at one point it held 32,000. For fourteen months during 1864 and 1865, more than 45,000 Union soldiers were confined here, of which almost one-third died from disease, malnutrition, overcrowding, or exposure.

Deteriorating economic conditions in the Confederacy, coupled with an inadequate transportation system and the need to concentrate resources on the army, resulted in woefully meager housing, food, clothing, and medical care for the prisoners. Each man had only a few feet of living space. His only shelter might be a shirt spread over some branches. Sanitary facilities were nonexistent.

Water was in such short supply in August 1864 that prisoners were desperately praying for it. After a heavy rain, an old spring began to flow again. Thankful captives named it Providence Spring.

When Gen. William Tecumseh Sherman occupied Atlanta on September 2, 1864, Confederate authorities moved most of the Andersonville prisoners to camps in coastal Georgia and South Carolina. The prison ceased to exist when the war ended in May 1865.

Clara Barton, whose humanitarian efforts included providing medical supplies, aid, and care for Union troops, was sent to Andersonville in July and August of 1865 to ascertain the whereabouts of missing Union soldiers. She was able to locate and mark the graves of all but 460 of the men who died there.

After the war, the prison grounds reverted to private ownership, but in 1890 the area was purchased by the Department of the Grand Army of the Republic (GAR), a Union veterans organization. It was later sold to the Women's Relief Corps, the national auxiliary of the GAR, for $1.00.

It was the Women's Relief Corps that made many improvements, planted trees, erected monuments, and created the memorial park. They donated it to the people of the United States in 1910, after which it was administered by the War Department and the Department of the Army before being made a national historic site in 1970.

The Visitors Center houses a museum containing exhibits about Andersonville and Civil War prisons in general, the systems of prisoner exchange and parole used during the Civil War, and records of individual prisoners. You'll be oriented to the site by an audiovisual presentation as well as by relief maps. A brochure and audiotape are available for a self-guided tour. The Prisoner of War Museum chronicles American wars from the Revolution to Vietnam.

Wayside exhibits along the tour route recreate the harsh conditions that existed. Sometimes costumed guides demonstrate the brutal methods that were used to control prisoners.

The most poignant event is the annual Memorial Day celebration, when 16,000 American flags fly throughout the cemetery.

12-28-07

The nearby restored Civil War village of Andersonville is a tiny, sleepy hamlet where time seems to have stood still. Civil War prisoners arrived here by rail and were marched the quarter mile to the prison. The town became the supply center for the prison as well as the headquarters of its notorious commander, Capt. Henry Wirz—later hanged by the federal government for war crimes.

Andersonville's Welcome Center and Drummer Boy Civil War Museum are housed in the old railway depot. Authentic documents, guns, swords, flags, uniforms, and other Civil War accoutrements are displayed, and visitor information and souvenirs are available.

Easterlin Country Store, along quiet, shady Church Street, contains antiques, collectibles, and books. Also on Church Street are arts and crafts and antique shops, small churches, and an ancient cemetery. St. James Church, although built of logs, is an architectural gem designed by Cramm and Ferguson, architects of the Cathedral of St. John the Divine in New York City. Nearby is a pioneer farm park with a log cabin, barn, farm animals, sugarcane mill, and syrup kettle.

Annually, on Memorial Day weekend and the first weekend in October, the town hosts the Andersonville Historic Fair, which features a Civil War encampment and skirmish between Confederate and Union troops; demonstrations by old-time craftsmen such as blacksmiths, potters, glassblowers, and quilters; and performances by square dancers, cloggers,

The eloquent row upon row of headstones at Andersonville

and military bands. A large flea market draws bargain hunters from miles around.

Accommodations can be found in a charming bed and breakfast called A Place Away—two suites in a converted sharecroppers' cottage at 110 Oglethorpe Street. The small town-owned RV campground provides a woodsy environment with concrete parking pads as well as electric, water, and sewer hookups.

Two miles south of Andersonville on State 49 is historic Trebor Plantation, established in 1833 by Robert Hodges. He was a Confederate chaplain to prisoners at Andersonville Prison and also provided food to the prison. The plantation house, immortalized in McKinley Kantor's Pulitzer Prize–winning *Andersonville*, is Greek Revival with Edwardian adaptations. Original hand-planed boards remain on the front facade and in two parlors. The grounds are dotted with traditional plantation dependencies (outbuildings) in the process of restoration. You can tour the house and grounds together or separately.

Also south of Andersonville is Pecan World, on Old Andersonville Highway off State 49, which offers the delicious nuts in every form imaginable. During the mid-October to December harvest season, you can tour the orchards, the processing and cleaning plant, and gift shop.

Continue on State 49 to Americus, located in the heart of Sumter County. Americus has a large historic district of antebellum and Victorian buildings. Brochures for walking and driving tours are available from the Chamber of Commerce at 400 West Lamar Street. You can also visit the Lindbergh Memorial at Souther Airfield on State 49, site of Charles Lindbergh's first solo flight in 1923.

Americus is blessed with several outstanding accommodations. The restored 1892 Windsor Hotel, 125 West Lamar Street, is an architectural masterpiece, one of only two

Georgia hotels listed in the National Trust for Historic Preservation's Historic Hotels of America. The Italianate style is embellished with a Flemish stepped roof and a Romanesque tower. If you don't stay there, at least eat at the restaurant and take a quick tour.

The bounty of magnificent antebellum and Victorian homes lends itself to bed and breakfast accommodations. The Cottage Inn is an elegant Victorian estate just outside of town on State 49. A charming Louisiana-style raised cottage is the centerpiece of The Guerry House/Springhill Plantation, 723 McGarrah Street, where guest accommodations are in two historic outbuildings. Avid Civil War buffs and reenacters, the owners host periodic reenactments on the grounds.

Take a detour west on US 280 to Plains, former president Jimmy Carter's hometown, now the Jimmy Carter National Historic Site. Visitors can take a self-guided tour with information from the Georgia Visitor Information Center, on US 280 just outside of town. Carter's first campaign headquarters is housed in the Depot Museum, where pictures and memorabilia from his boyhood through his presidency are displayed. A fifteen-minute video shows the Carters giving a tour of their private residence. You might even catch a glimpse of the famous duo bicycling through town.

Across the street is the delightful pink Victorian Plains Bed & Breakfast Inn, 100 West Church Street. Carter's mother, Miss Lillian, roomed there as a single woman and shortly after her marriage.

Return to Americus and take US 280 east toward Cordele. Before you reach town, you'll come to 8,500-acre Lake Blackshear, home of Veterans Memorial State Park. In addition to a museum devoted to Georgia veterans, the park features a pool, beach, boating, fishing, picnicking, camping, and cabins.

Cordele is known as the "Watermelon Capital of the World." The historic downtown—designated on the National Register of Historic Places—served as the state capital during the last days of the Confederacy. A self-guided walking tour brochure is available from the Chamber of Commerce, 302 East Sixteenth Avenue. Cordele's Watermelon Days is a July event featuring watermelon-eating and seed-spitting contests.

Although not officially on the Andersonville Trail, Vienna, just north of Cordele on US 41, is worth a visit. A brochure for a driving tour of sixty historic sites is available at the Chamber of Commerce, at 204-A West Union Street.

Native son Walter F. George was a prominent Georgia legislator who served as a U.S. senator for more than thirty-five years. He is best known as the architect of the North Atlantic Treaty Organization. The Walter F. George Law Office and Museum, located in George Busbee Park on State 215, houses artifacts and memorabilia from his career.

Ellis Brothers Pecans, on State 215 one mile east of I-75 at exit 36, is a processing plant that offers confectionery tours.

What really puts Vienna on the map is its renowned Big Pig Jig (Georgia's official barbecue cooking championship), held the second weekend in October. Named one of the Top 100 Events in America by the American Bus Association and one of the Top Ten Events in the Southeast, the event draws more than 115 teams competing in ribs, shoulder, whole hog, and Brunswick stew categories. We've judged both showmanship and ribs in this fun-filled cook-off for several years and can testify that the event is finger-lickin', foot-stompin' fun. Winners advance to the national competition, called Memphis in May. The event also features musical entertainment, arts and crafts, and a carnival. Another cook-off extravaganza is the Southern Wild Game and Fish Cookoff, held on the same site the second weekend in March.

It may seem like going from the sublime to the ridiculous to begin with a floral tribute at Massee Lane Gardens, then proceed to the tragic history at Andersonville, only to end up at the Big Pig Jig in Vienna, but that only points out that the Andersonville Trail offers something for everyone.

In the Area

Americus/Sumter County Chamber of Commerce, 400 West Lamar Street, Americus, GA 31709, 912-924-2646.

Andersonville Local Welcome Center, Old Railroad Depot, Andersonville, GA 31711, 912-924-2558.

Cordele-Crisp County Chamber of Commerce, 302 East Sixteenth Avenue, Cordele, GA 31015, 912-273-3526.

Georgia Visitors Information Center, US 280, Plains, GA 31780, 912-824-7477.

Vienna-Dooly County Chamber of Commerce, 204-A West Union Street, Vienna, GA 31092, 912-268-4554.

12-29-99

2 ~

Antebellum Trail

Getting there: Take State 22, US 129, or US 441.

Highlights: *Macon's Cherry Blossom Festival, the Uncle Remus Museum, eating fresh fish at the Oconee Cafe, and the magnificent State Botanical Garden and Conservatory in Athens.*

Rambling through peaceful rural tapestries, State 22, US 129, and US 441 form an antique necklace connecting Macon and Athens—its links, the jewels of Old Clinton, Milledgeville, Eatonton, Madison, and Watkinsville. Known as the Antebellum Trail, this 100-mile pathway lends itself to short getaways.

It's easy to follow the trail. The silhouette of a whimsical pre–Civil War lady—"Auntie Bellum"—graces all the road markers. Leave yourself ample time to sample the trail's enchantments in a leisurely fashion. At least three days and two nights are needed to do the area any justice. Four to five days would be perfect.

Antebellum refers to the time preceding the Civil War. Although that was a time of grace and plenty for a few, the period has become the stereotypical representation of the Old South.

Spared by Gen. William Tecumseh Sherman's troops during his infamous March to the Sea, numerous architectural marvels along the trail survive to remind visitors of this idyllic era.

We begin our tour in Macon—the city of white columns and cherry blossoms—so named because of its abundance of antebellum structures and its profusion of pink springtime blooms. With 180,000 Yoshino cherry trees, Macon boasts more than Washington, D.C. The city is at its showiest during the March Cherry Blossom Festival.

The original city fathers provided for the generous parks and wide avenues that survive today. A booming economy in the nineteenth century allowed wealthy planters and businessmen to build opulent mansions in town. Various stories circulate about why the city was spared during the Civil War, but the result is captivating to resident and visitor alike.

One of the most extravagant survivors is the Hay House, 934 Georgia Avenue. Owned by only two families in its history, it is now operated by the Georgia Trust for Historic Preservation. A national landmark, the mansion was built in the Italian Renaissance style during the 1850s and incorporated such unheard-of amenities as indoor hot and cold plumbing, an elevator, an intercom, and a ventilation system. The magnificent red-brick villa, perched overlooking downtown, contains twenty-four antique-filled rooms.

As fascinating as are the sumptuous furnishings and museum pieces, more astonishing is a superiority in workmanship that is almost impossible to find these days. Even marble mantels and elaborately embossed cornices, medallions, and moldings pale beside the intricate trompe l'oeil wall and ceiling paintings, only now rediscovered after years of being covered by layers of paint and wallpaper.

The Old Cannonball House, 856 Mulberry Street, was the only Macon building struck during the Union attack in 1864. The mortar round crashed through a column of the Greek Revival home and landed in the parlor, where it remains today. The house, which is open to the public, has several rooms furnished as replicas of rooms at old Wesleyan College, the country's first woman's college and home of the first national sororities. The detached brick kitchen and servants' quarters form a Confederate Museum.

Georgia's beloved poet Sidney Lanier was born in Macon in 1842 while his parents were visiting his grandparents. Lanier lost his health while serving as a Confederate soldier; he died at thirty-nine. Memorabilia from his life is displayed at Lanier Cottage, 935 High Street.

Harriet Tubman, creator and moving force behind the underground railroad, which spirited slaves north during the Civil War, was a Macon native. The Harriet Tubman Historical and Cultural Museum, 340 Walnut Street, displays art and artifacts about her life and the underground railroad movement. An arresting mural records the 400-year journey of Blacks from Africa to contemporary America.

City Hall served as the temporary capital of Georgia during 1864 and 1865. The last session of Georgia's Confederate Congress met here. A Monument to Women of the Confederacy, one of the first in the country, stands on the Avenue of Flags. Another Confederate Monument stands at Second Street and Cotton Avenue.

You could spend days on foot just wandering the streets of Macon's six historic districts using brochures for Three Historic Walking Tours to Discover Old Macon or by horse and carriage with Sidney's Old South Historic Tours.

The ornate ballroom of the Hay House in Macon

In this century, Macon has had a rich Black musical tradition. The Pleasant Hill Historic District is one of the first Black neighborhoods listed on the National Register of Historic Places. It was the childhood home of Otis Redding, Little Richard Penniman, and Lena Horne. Macon's WIBB-AM is where James Brown got his recording break; the historic Douglass Theater, currently undergoing restoration, hosted Bessie Smith, Cab Calloway, and Count Basie, among others.

The variety of Macon's architecture creates a photographer's paradise. Visit the Greek Revival Woodruff House on Bond Street by appointment, or tour the restored 1884 Grand Opera House, 651 Mulberry Street, which boasts one of the largest stages in the nation.

In keeping with the antebellum character of Macon, you might like to stay in a historic bed and breakfast. The sumptuous 1842 Inn, 353 College Street, offers luxurious accommodations in the grand antebellum Greek Revival mansion or in its adjoining Victorian cottage.

Just north of I-16 and east of downtown off State 57 is the Ocmulgee National Monument/Visitor Center/Museum, where several Indian mounds, a reconstructed ceremonial earth lodge, and the movie *People of the Macon Plateau* trace the Native American history of the area back 12,000 years. The park contains 683 acres of nature trails.

West of town between State 74 and US 80 is Lake Tobesofkee, which offers numerous water sports, camping, picnicking, and tennis, as well as frequent horse shows.

As hard as it is to tear yourself away from Macon, you'd be cheating yourself if you didn't continue along the Antebellum Trail.

Not far north up US 129 is Old Clinton, "the town that time forgot." The lack of modern development has preserved the New England influence brought by early settlers in 1808 when Clinton was the county seat. Streets, laid out in a gridiron pattern around a central square, were named for early American heroes.

By 1820, Clinton was the fourth largest town in Georgia. Unfortunately, several Civil War skirmishes changed the town forever. Federal raiders plundered and pillaged, stealing or destroying more than a third of the town, including residences, the school, churches, and the tannery.

The Old Clinton Historical Society is working to restore and preserve Clinton. About thirty historic buildings and the cemetery of the period 1808–30 survive. Self-guided tours are free. Guided tours can be arranged. At Old Clinton Roadside Park, you can see huge granite outcroppings marking the Piedmont fall line.

Continue on US 129 to Gray, then take State 22 north to Milledgeville. The town began life in 1803 as Georgia's third capital, which it remained for sixty years. During that prosperous time, fine homes, churches, schools, and other public buildings burgeoned. The present-day historic district features more than twenty architectural landmarks as well as countless residential treasures.

The best way to survey Milledgeville is by a two-hour tour on the town trolley, which originates from the Milledgeville Tourism and Trade office at 200 West Hancock Street. The trolley operates two days a week, and entrance to several historic buildings is included in the tour.

 The Old State Capitol Building, 201 East Greene Street, which served the legislature from 1807 to 1868, now functions as classrooms and administrative offices for Georgia Military College as well as a museum of early Milledgeville and college memorabilia.

One of the finest examples of Greek Revival architecture in Georgia is the 1838 Old Governor's Mansion, 120 South

Clark Street—the last of three Greek Revival structures in town. The lower floors are open for tours; the upper story serves as offices for the president of Georgia College.

Across the street is the Museum and Archives of Georgia Education, 131 South Clark Street, which presents the history of education in the state through photographs and memorabilia.

On the Georgia College campus is the Flannery O'Connor Room, dedicated to the popular southern author. Although she preferred Alabama, she was born in Milledgeville, and her mother still lives in a Victorian cottage that is pointed out on the tour.

Headquarters of Allied Arts, the Marlor House, 200 North Wayne Street, presents rotating exhibits. The 1812 Stetson-Sanford House, on West Hancock Street, received national acclaim for architectural design and beautiful workmanship. Saint Stephen's Episcopal Church is architecturally interesting, but its claim to fame is that it served as a stable for Union troops during the Civil War.

Mara's Tara, 330 West Green Street, is a bed and breakfast in an elegant Greek Revival home.

From Milledgeville, turn north on US 441 to see the rest of the Antebellum Trail. Take a short detour south of town to the Lockerly Arboretum, where you can examine wild plant life from trails and wooden bridges that wander over fifty acres. Returning to your northerly route, you'll come to Lake Sinclair, a 15,000-acre lake with more than 500 miles of shoreline.

Eatonton boasts two major authors—Joel Chandler Harris, creator of the Uncle Remus tales, and Alice Walker, author of *The Color Purple* and *The Temple of My Familiar*.

The town was laid out in 1808 surrounding the public square and courthouse. In homage to Harris, a brightly dressed Brer Rabbit statue surveys the courthouse lawn and passersby.

On US 441 at the south edge of town is the Uncle Remus Museum, constructed from two former slave cabins similar to the one occupied by Uncle Remus. Colorful painted scenes depict southern plantation life that probably never existed, where everyone was happy and carefree. Shadowboxes containing delicate wood carvings of "de critters" encircle the walls. A crude fireplace is surrounded by memorabilia of the era. Of particular interest are first editions of Harris's works, his handwritten letters, clothing items, and other mementos. The portrait *Uncle Remus and the Little Boy* dominates the room. The museum is located in Turner Park, so named because it was the homeplace of Joseph Sidney Turner, on whom the Little Boy was modeled.

Harris once lived in a small cottage with his mother behind The Bronson House. This stately main house accented with fluted Doric columns is now a museum. Brochures for a walking tour of Eatonton are available from the Chamber of Commerce.

Two historic Victorian homes, the 1895 Crockett House and 1888 Rosewood, offer bed and breakfast accommodations.

At US 441/US 129 north of Eatonton, on the grounds of the Rock Eagle 4-H Club Center, is a marvel rivaling the Egyptian pyramids. The Rock Eagle Effigy is a stone mound, or tumulus, in the shape of a gigantic prone bird with outstretched wings. Its wingspan measures 102 feet, it is 120 feet from head to tail, and its body rises 10 feet above the surrounding surface. Construction is of various-sized quartz boulders thought to have been transported from as far as 100 miles away. Historians and archaeologists speculate that the effigy is at least 6,000 years old, making it older than the pyramids. Its use was probably religious. The best view of the effigy is from an observation tower. Public facilities include a 110-acre lake, picnic areas, boats, and fishing facilities.

Located between Eatonton and Madison is Lake Oconee, a 19,000-acre recreational lake with almost 400 miles of shoreline and three large parks. A wildlife preserve, four marinas, public access ramps, a hotel, and luxury homesites are attracting tourists in droves. Folks drive for miles, even from Atlanta, to eat fresh fish at the Oconee Cafe, 516 Harmony Road.

Founded in 1809, graceful Madison was once called "the most cultured and aristocratic town on the stage route from Charleston to New Orleans." Prospering from the cotton economy, wealthy planters built not only vast plantations but also elegant town homes. Most of the existing notable architecture dates between 1830 and 1860.

Known also as "the town Sherman refused to burn," Madison was spared during the March to the Sea. Various reasons are given for saving the town. One is that Sen. Joshua Hill, who had not voted for secession, made a personal plea to Sherman. Unfortunately, an 1869 fire destroyed much of the commercial sector. New brick structures of the Italianate Victorian style were built around the town square, where they continue to prosper, revitalized by Georgia's Main Street project. A two-story 1890s hotel is crammed with a treasure trove of antique shops, such as Utterly Yours-Washington Street Antiques, 140 West Washington Street.

An exceptional example of residential architecture is Heritage Hall, 277 South Main Street, headquarters of the Morgan County Historical Society. In addition to a tour of the beautifully restored and furnished 1825 Greek Revival home, you can watch a slide presentation orienting you to the town's historic structures, including a superb collection of Victorian homes built after the Civil War. Many of these treasures are open for tours in May and December.

18

Victorian gingerbread decorates a home in Madison

Pick up a brochure and audiotape for a self-guided tour of 100 historic buildings from the Chamber of Commerce, 115 East Jefferson Street. One of the oldest homes in town is the Cornelius Vason House, 549 Old Post Road, which was once a stagecoach inn.

You'll want to make time to visit the Madison-Morgan Cultural Center, 434 South Main Street, housed in an 1895 Romanesque Revival schoolhouse—one of the first graded (as opposed to one-room) brick schoolhouses in the South. Two renovated classrooms house a History Museum showcasing decorative arts, artifacts, and interpretive information. Another classroom is restored and furnished as it would have been at the turn of the century. Other rooms are adapted as galleries for changing art exhibits. The newest addition is the Morgan County African-American Museum.

The school's unusual apse-shaped, heart-pine and plaster auditorium still contains the original seating, chandelier, and woodwork. It is used for performing arts all year, including Madison's renowned Theater Festival in August.

Madison boasts several historic bed and breakfasts. The Brady Inn, 250 North Second Street, occupies two connected Victorian cottages encircled by rocker-filled porches. The Boat House, 383 Porter Street, built in 1850, was named because it was the home of a former sea captain. Antique lovers, the owners have packed their home with Victorian delights. Turn of the Century Bed and Breakfast, 450 Pine Street, is an antique-filled Victorian home featuring a wraparound porch. Burnett House, 317 Old Post Road, is eclectically furnished and sports an extensive art collection.

Nearby, Hard Labor Creek State Park, the largest state park in Georgia, offers swimming, fishing, boating, camping, and picnicking. Horse stables, trails, and an eighteen-hole golf course make this an exceptional park.

Mockingbird Forge, in a restored 1900 depot in Farmington on US 441, provides demonstrations of almost-lost skills by local artisans—a blacksmith, glassblower, potter, and woodworker. The work of several native artists is on display and for sale.

Watkinsville was once considered for the site of the University of Georgia. However, the powers that be decided that the existence of the Eagle Tavern made the town "too frivolous an atmosphere for studious young gentlemen."

Originally known as Fort Edwards, the tavern, on US 441, was built to protect settlers from Indians. The upstairs had only loopholes from which guns could be fired. Eventually, the tavern grew to a rambling sixteen-room hotel. Now restored to its original four-room size, the tavern serves as Watkinsville's Welcome Center. The downstairs is furnished as a tavern, the upstairs as an inn. One room contains artifacts dug up during restoration.

The town's historic district contains thirty-eight structures representing several late-nineteenth- and early-twentieth-century styles. A network of old Indian and pioneer trails radiates from the town. Five miles away is Elder Mill Bridge, on State 15 at Rose Creek, one of the few covered bridges remaining in the state and one of even fewer in use. Rivendell, 3581 South Barnett Shoals Road near Watkinsville, is a bed and breakfast in a contemporary house in a woodsy, country setting.

We complete our tour of the Antebellum Trail in Athens. The Classic City—named for its predecessor in Greece—is not only the home of the University of Georgia (UGA), the nation's first state-chartered university, it is also the site of America's first garden club. The city contains myriad remnants of antebellum opulence where massive-columned grand mansions are surrounded by magnolia-shaded formal gardens.

Start your tour with the Church-Waddel-Brumby House, a restored Federal period house at 280 East Dougherty Street, which serves as the Athens Welcome Center. Built in 1820, the house is believed to be the oldest surviving residence in Athens.

An 1845 Greek Revival home, the Taylor-Grady House, at 634 Prince Avenue, is flanked by thirteen Doric columns—representing the thirteen colonies—bound together by exquisite iron tracery. As a student, Henry W. Grady, journalist, orator, and editor of the *Atlanta Constitution*, lived in the house. He was instrumental in reconciling the North and South after the Civil War and coined the phrase "New South."

One of the most-cherished Civil War relics in Athens is the Double-barreled Cannon, on Hancock Street. The theory behind the design of this one-of-a-kind weapon was that each barrel would be loaded with a cannonball connected to the other by a chain. When fired, the balls and chain would sweep across the battlefield, mowing down wide swaths of the enemy.

Unfortunately, when tested, these were the reported results. The cannonballs "plowed up an acre of ground, tore up a cornfield, mowed down saplings, and the chain broke, the balls going in opposite directions, one of the balls killed a cow in a distant field, while the other knocked down the chimney from a log cabin. The observers scattered as though the entire Yankee army had turned loose in that vicinity."

Although the lauded "super-weapon" failed to perform as hoped, it is still a monument to the ingenuity of its inventor—Athens house builder John Gilleland. It sits in a special park on the City Hall lawn, facing north—"just in case."

Athens boasts a Tree That Owns Itself. Professor W. H. Jackson deeded the tree eight feet of land on all sides at the corner of Dearing and Finley Streets because he enjoyed its shade so much.

The U.S. Navy Supply Corps Museum, Prince and Oglethorpe Avenues, is located on the campus of the U.S. Navy Supply Corps School. The museum displays ship models, historic uniforms, navy equipment, and galley gear, and contains archives that include photos, official records, and cruise books. Also on the campus is Winnie Davis Memorial Hall, dedicated to the daughter of Confederate president Jefferson Davis.

The Classic City is blessed with an abundance of well-preserved ornamental ironwork—a decorative reminder of the nineteenth century. Much of what you see around the city was manufactured locally at the Athens Foundry, the original site of which is now part of the Quality Inn History Village.

Nothing symbolizes the University of Georgia more than its ironwork Arch. Gateway to the campus, its three columns represent wisdom, justice, and moderation. Current students and alumni might be amused to know that when the arch and associated fence were erected in 1858, their more plebeian purpose was to keep freely wandering livestock and domestic animals off the campus. Some other easily accessible examples of ironwork on campus include the garden benches, stairways, and balcony balustrades in the Old North Campus Historic District, the lighting standards on the Broad Street Quadrangle, and the porch balustrade featuring cast medallions with portraits of famous poets and statesmen at the School of Law.

However, it is the use of ornate ironwork in home embellishment—particularly porches and balconies—that draws the most interest from passersby. John C. Waters, professor of historic preservation at the University of Georgia, has compiled a walking tour brochure that highlights some of the most spectacular examples. The brochure can be obtained from the Convention and Visitors Bureau. Use it in conjunction with the bureau's pamphlet "Athens of Old," which contains more complete descriptions of the buildings.

The Founders Memorial Garden, a small formal garden on the grounds of the university, commemorates the first garden club in America. The early 1800s house is furnished with period pieces.

Everything in Athens isn't old. The Georgia Museum of Art, on the university campus, houses an impressive permanent collection and hosts visiting exhibits. The Butts-Mehre Heritage Hall, Lumpkin and Pinecrest Streets near the university, is a strikingly modern museum showcasing the athletic accomplishments of UGA students.

A magnificent new addition to the city is the State Botanical Garden of Georgia, 2450 Milledge Avenue, where a 10,000-square-foot conservatory displays tropical and semitropical plants. The 293-acre preserve is located in a forest along the Oconee River set amid dramatic gorgelike ravines and spring-fed streams and native plant life of the region.

Two exquisite places to eat in Athens are Trumps at the Georgian, 247 East Washington Street, and Harry Bisset's New Orleans Cafe, 279 East Broad Street.

Although no bed and breakfasts are located in Athens, there are several nearby. The Hardeman/Hutchens House is a pleasant farmhouse at 5335 Lexington Road (US 78) east of town. The Old Winterville Inn, due east of town at 108 South Main Street in nearby Winterville, offers one splendid suite.

Christmas is celebrated in a big way along the Antebellum Trail. Just imagine the magnificent antebellum and Victorian mansions opulently bedecked for the festive season. Macon, Madison, and Athens offer spectacular Christmas events, including candlelight tours.

Contact the Madison-Morgan Chamber of Commerce for *A Guide to Georgia's Antebellum Trail* or a calendar of activities along the trail.

As you travel all or part of the Antebellum Trail, you'll be drawn in to the romance, beauty, and mystery of the Old

South, but you'll also enjoy a variety of craft fairs, music festivals, seasonal celebrations, and other cultural events.

In the Area

Athens Convention and Visitors Bureau, P.O. Box 948, Athens, GA 30603, 706-546-1805.

Athens Local Welcome Center, 280 East Dougherty Street, Athens, GA 30603, 706-353-1820.

Eagle Tavern Local Welcome Center, US 441, Watkinsville, GA 30677, 706-769-5197.

Macon-Bibb County Convention and Visitors Bureau, Terminal Station, 200 Cherry Street, Macon, GA 31201, 912-743-3401.

Macon I-75 Local Welcome Center, I-75S, Macon, GA 31208, 912-745-2668.

Madison-Morgan County Chamber of Commerce, 115 East Jefferson Street, Madison, GA 30650, 706-342-4454.

Milledgeville-Baldwin Tourism and Trade, 200 West Hancock Street, Milledgeville, GA 31061, 912-452-4687.

3 ~

Blue and Gray Trail

Getting there: Start with LaFayette at US 27 and State 136.

Highlights: *Civil War battlefields and Confederate cemeteries, the romantic English-style Barnsley Gardens, The General—survivor of the Great Locomotive Chase, the antebellum homes of Roswell, and Atlanta's Cyclorama.*

The sun shines gently over rolling hills. Wildflowers poke their brightly colored heads through the thick carpet of grass. Motes of dust play in the sunbeams filtering through the canopy of nearby pines to mottle the forest floor with pools of dancing light. Birds swoop and soar, their cheerful songs filling the silence.

You can hardly imagine that once rifles cracked, cannon boomed, terrified men and animals screamed and died. These battlefields and cemetery sites are reminders of the bitter conflict between brother Americans.

The Civil War wasn't just about slavery; for politicians and the well-to-do, it was very much about states' rights. But what was it about to the common foot soldier? A Yankee soldier asked a Confederate why he was fighting. His answer was, "Because you're down here." The sites on the Blue and Gray Trail and around the state are testaments to those who fought and died here.

No matter what you call it—the Civil War, the War Between the States, the War of Northern Aggression, or our personal favorite, the Recent Unpleasantness—and regardless of your political feelings about the war, haunting memories of the great American tragedy pervade these sites. Despite their dark past, these peaceful spots are ideal places to learn history or just have a pleasant afternoon stroll or picnic.

Northwest Georgia was a significant player in the unfolding of the Civil War long before Union Gen. William Tecumseh Sherman thrust into the state on his march toward Atlanta and on to the sea. The Western & Atlantic Railroad, the Confederacy's most vital transportation artery, ran from the Tennessee border to Atlanta, feeding munitions and supplies to battlefronts as far away as Virginia. This corridor had to be destroyed if the Union was to prevail.

The following story sets the stage for exploring the fifty sites along the 150-mile Blue and Gray Trail. One of the Civil War's most daring espionage escapades was an attempt to destroy the Georgia rail link. James Andrews, a civilian, black marketeer, and Union spy, along with twenty-three Union soldiers stole the Confederate locomotive *The General* from Big Shanty, Georgia, with the intent of disrupting rail service to the Confederacy. Their mission was to tear up track, cut telegraph lines, and burn bridges. That their plan failed was due to the quick and persistent actions of the train's conductor, William Fuller.

In early April 1862, Andrews and his men slipped over the border from Tennessee and quietly made their way to

Marietta. On April 12, dressed in unobtrusive civilian cloth-ing, they bought tickets to various destinations and boarded the passenger train pulled by *The General*. Everyone disem-barked when the train stopped at the Lacy Hotel in Big Shanty for a breakfast break. Andrews and company unhooked the passenger cars and hijacked the engine and three boxcars. Their exploit was doubly daring because Camp McDonald, a training camp for Confederate soldiers, was just across the tracks.

Fuller, engineer Jeff Cain, and shop foreman Anthony Murphy first chased the locomotive on foot and then on a handcar. Refusing to be defeated, they commandeered the freight engine *Yonah* and continued the chase. Near Kingston, Fuller exchanged the *Yonah* for the smaller, faster *William R. Smith*, continuing to gain on *The General*.

Despite frequent stops for water and wood, Andrews had enough time to cut some telegraph wires and take up some track, leaving Fuller and his men once again on foot. At Adairsville, Fuller was offered the fast-moving freight loco-motive *The Texas*. Because the pursuers didn't have time to turn the locomotive around, they ended up chasing the raiders in reverse. However, that turned out to be a blessing. To thwart the pursuers, Andrews uncoupled first one, than another of the boxcars. Fuller simply coupled them onto his locomotive and continued the pursuit.

As the chase continued through Calhoun and Dalton, Fuller picked up ten heavily armed Confederate soldiers and telegraph operator Ed Henderson, who was able to send a message alerting the Confederate army to the situation. Al-though Andrews attempted to burn bridges, a slow, misting rain foiled his plans. So relentlessly were the hijackers being pursued that they didn't have time to tear up any more track, just some easily removed crossties.

At Ringgold, only a few miles from the Tennessee border, *The General* stopped cold on a hill. After all, the pursuers had changed locomotives several times, but *The General* had gone the entire distance. It was worn out. The hijackers fled into the woods. Some were captured; others escaped. Of those captured, some were paroled; others, despite subsequent jail breaks, were later hanged in Atlanta. They became the first recipients of the Congressional Medal of Honor. Andrews, a civilian, wasn't eligible.

The Great Locomotive Chase has spawned dozens of books and two movies, one in 1926 with Buster Keaton and the other in 1956 with Fess Parker. Recently, the U.S. Postal Service honored *The General* with a postage stamp. Many of the sites made famous by the Great Locomotive Chase are prominently featured on the Blue and Gray Trail.

There are so many attractions on the trail that you could easily spend a week, or two long weekends, exploring it. It makes sense to survey the trail in approximately the order in which events happened, so we suggest you start with LaFayette at US 27 and State 136. Visit John B. Gordon Hall (on US 27), which Confederate Gen. Braxton Bragg used as his headquarters for a week before the Battle at Chickamauga, and McLemore's Cove (on State 193), where attempts were made to trap and destroy the Union army.

The General, *star of the Great Locomotive Chase*

Next, go north on US 27 to the Chickamauga/Chattanooga National Military Park. The largest, oldest, and most-visited military park in the country, it celebrated its 104th birthday on August 19, 1994. Straddling the border of North Georgia and Tennessee, the two sites give you an excellent overview of the connection between the battles and their far-reaching consequences. The Cherokee called this area "Thunder in the Ground." Despite their own turbulent history and eventual forcible removal, they could never have envisioned the thunderous battle that was to come.

Chickamauga was the site of one of the Confederacy's greatest victories. On September 19-20, 1863, fighting for control of the LaFayette Road, 35,000 of 120,000 soldiers lost their lives. Unfortunately, the South's failure to follow up led to the loss at Chattanooga several months later, which opened the way for Sherman's penetration into the Deep South during the summer of 1864.

The Chickamauga section of the battlefield park covers 8,000 acres and boasts a new ultramodern and comprehensive visitors center with several exhibits, a bookstore, a gift shop, and a multimedia presentation describing the battle. The most popular exhibit is the Fuller Gun Collection. With 355 shoulder arms dating from the Revolutionary War to World War II, it includes one of the most extensive assemblies anywhere of Civil War guns.

Get a map and/or an audiotape for an eight-mile self-guided tour of the military park. You might drive, but the level site is perfect for touring on foot, by bicycle, or even on horseback. Numerous monuments and historical markers explain the progression of the battle.

One of the most beautiful bed and breakfasts in the state is in the hamlet of Chickamauga on State 341. The 1847 Greek Revival Gordon-Lee Mansion, 217 Cove Road, was commandeered by federal forces under Gen. William Rosecrans, and its magnificent library was pressed into service as an operating room. In addition to offering luxurious accommodations, the house now boasts a small Civil War museum open during the summer. At Fort Oglethorpe, right across the street from the Chickamauga visitors center, is another charming bed and breakfast—Captains Quarters, at 13 Barnhardt Circle. Also located at the fort is the Sixth Cavalry Museum.

You may elect to omit the portion of the park in Tennessee. However, we suggest that in order to understand the Atlanta Campaign you follow US 27 north and cross over the border to Chattanooga. Significant Civil War sites there include Point Park at the Lookout Mountain Battlefield, Chattanooga National Cemetery, Andrews Raiders Monument, Missionary Ridge, Confederama, Cravens House, Read House/Crutchfield House, Medal of Honor Museum, and Reflection Riding.

Once Chattanooga was firmly in Union hands on November 25, 1863, Gen. Ulysses Grant sent Sherman to capture Atlanta and cut off the Confederacy's transportation and supplies once and for all. Sherman described his operation as "a beehive full of bees ready to swarm on Atlanta." However, Confederate resistance was so great that Atlanta didn't fall until September 1864—more than nine months later.

Return to Georgia via US 41/US 76 and proceed to Ringgold. During the Battle of Ringgold Gap in 1863, Confederates around the old Ringgold Depot managed to maintain control long enough for the main army to establish a defense line around Dalton. General Grant occupied the Whitman House and upon leaving offered to pay the family for use of their home in U.S. dollars, but they refused. The Old Stone Baptist Church, built in 1849, still has its original altar and pews despite the fact that it was the center of some heavy action. A relief map on US 41 illustrates the events from May 7 through September 2, 1864. Remember that it was in Ringgold that the Andrews Raiders had to abandon *The General*, the monument

Chickamauga/Chattanooga Military Park includes monuments to both Union and Confederate soldiers

of which is located on Ooltewah Road, two miles north of town.

The brochure "Battlefields and Backroads: A Self-Guided Photo Tour" lists several significant landmarks in Fort Oglethorpe and Ringgold along with tips for taking good pictures. The brochure is published by Catoosa County in conjunction with the Appalachian Regional Commission and the Tennessee Valley Authority.

Continue south on US 41/US 76 to Tunnel Hill. Turn left off US 41 onto Oak Street. At the Tunnel Hill historic markers, continue straight onto Clisbe Austin Drive and pass through a covered bridge; the tunnel is on the left. The 1849 underpass was the first one south of the Mason-Dixon Line. Control of the tunnel was important because it was an important north-south route as well as the only rail connection through the Appalachian barrier between the Atlantic coast and the western frontier. During the summer, it is almost hidden by kudzu.

In 1861, on his way to Montgomery, Alabama, for his inauguration as president of the Confederacy, Jefferson Davis rode through the tunnel and delivered a speech at the depot. Andrews and his Raiders passed through it during the Great Locomotive Chase in 1862. Several skirmishes took place at Tunnel Hill between September 1863 and March 1865.

After the battle of Chickamauga in 1863, the entire community of Tunnel Hill became a hospital for hundreds of wounded. Two cemeteries hold the remains of many Civil War veterans. One of the wounded was Confederate Gen. John Bell Hood, who was brought to the Clisbe Austin House, known as Meadowland, adjacent to the tunnel. The same house later served as Sherman's headquarters as he planned the Atlanta Campaign and the March to the Sea. The house is open for tours by prior arrangement.

As his Confederate troops were pushed south in 1864, Gen. Joseph Johnston requested permission to blow up the tunnel, but the plea must have gone astray because the request was never answered, causing Johnston to leave the tunnel intact when Sherman seized the town on May 7, 1864. Remains of entrenchments and gun emplacements are scattered along the ridge above the tunnel.

The tunnel was replaced with a newer one in 1928, but recently the Tunnel Hill Historic Foundation was formed to restore the old tunnel and create a historic park. A nearby site where Confederates camped is the scene of an annual reenactment to raise money for the project. During the September reenactment weekend, several historic homes and buildings in Tunnel Hill are open for tours.

South on US 41 at Rocky Face Ridge, another relief map describes Sherman and Johnston's movements on May 7–13, 1864.

More than 600 Union and 2,500 Confederate soldiers camped at various times at Prater's Mill—a three-story 1855 gristmill near Varnell on State 2. The grounds are always accessible, and the mill is open during the Prater's Mill Fairs in May and October.

Next south on US 41 is Dalton. Dug Gap Battle Park—a 2.5-acre park with 1,237 feet of Confederate breastworks—was the site of two successful Confederate stands, in which they were outnumbered ten to one.

In Dalton, the Blunt House, built in 1848 on Thornton Avenue, served as a Union hospital. The 1850s Western & Atlantic Depot on King Street, which served as a Confederate army ordnance depot, is now the Dalton Depot Restaurant. The former office of Crown Cotton Mill on Chattanooga Avenue, now Crown Gardens & Archives, houses Civil War relics, a bedspread museum, and research and genealogy material. The Confederate Cemetery, part of West Hill Cemetery on Emory Street, holds 421 Confederate and four Union unknown dead as well as a Confederate monument dedicated to soldiers who fell at Dalton, Rocky Face, Chickamauga, and Resaca.

Continuing south on US 41, you'll come to Resaca. The Resaca Confederate Cemetery, on Confederate Cemetery Road, was dedicated to Mary Green, a young girl who, with her sister and two former slaves, buried two fallen Confederate soldiers in their flower garden. Their father, Col. John Green, donated the land as the first Confederate cemetery. The Battle of Resaca—May 13–15, 1864—is reenacted annually. A relief map describes the battle and Johnston's evacuation on May 16.

South of Resaca at State 156 is Calhoun. Oakleigh, a mansion on Wall Street, was Sherman's headquarters during his advance through Calhoun. Today it is the home of the Gordon County Historical Society.

From Resaca, go south on State 156, then south on US 27 to Rome—named for its Italian counterpart because it is located on seven hills. Rome has its own Civil War hero. John Wisdom was in Alabama when by chance he overheard Union plans to march on Rome. He took off to warn his hometown, wearing out five horses and a mule as he made the sixty-seven-mile trip in less than nine hours. His feat earned him the title "Paul Revere of the South."

With the prior warning, Gen. Nathan Bedford Forrest was able to trick 1,800 Union cavalrymen into surrendering. Forrest had his 600 men march in circles around the federals, giving them the impression that there were many more Confederate troops. The Battle of Rome is reenacted each October.

The Noble Brothers Foundry in Rome, which provided cannon to the Confederacy, was destroyed in November 1864 by General Sherman. However, a lathe from the foundry is displayed at the Rome Visitor Center, on US 27 at Civic Center Hill.

There are graves of both Confederate and Union dead at Myrtle Hill Cemetery at South Broad and Myrtle Streets. Named for a profusion of crepe myrtles, the cemetery is located on one of the highest hills in town above the confluence of the Etowah and Oostanaula Rivers and affords a breathtaking view of Rome.

Cemetery monuments honor several well-known people. One venerates General Forrest for his role in saving Rome. Another commends Confederate women who cared for the wounded. Two notables buried there are Ellen Axson Wilson, wife of then President Woodrow Wilson, and Charles Graves, one of the last World War I soldiers buried and the recipient of the title America's Known Soldier.

The sanctuary of the 1849 First Presbyterian Church, at 101 East Third Street, remains unchanged since it was used as a hospital. Union troops quartered their horses in the 1852 St. Paul African-Methodist-Episcopal Church, at the corner of Sixth Avenue and West Second Street. Chieftans Museum, at 501 Riverside Parkway, contains Civil War artifacts such as weapons, books, letters, and clothing (see Chieftans Trail).

From US 27, take State 53 to the intersection of Martha Berry Highway and Veteran's Memorial Highway 53 Bypass. Union soldiers camped on the grounds of Oak Hill during the Battle for Rome. Residence of Martha Berry, founder of Berry College, the antebellum plantation museum home contains period furnishings and an extensive art collection.

Retrace State 53 north to State 140 and follow it east toward Adairsville to within 1.5 miles of I-75. Turn right onto Hall Station Road and go 5.5 miles to Barnsley Gardens Road.

Turn right and go two miles to the gardens. The signs are so tasteful and discreet, you need to keep a sharp eye out.

At Barnsley Gardens the romance of the antebellum period is reflected by the ruin of the 1842 mansion surrounded by thirty acres of English-style gardens. Carved from the Cherokee wilderness by Godfrey and Julia Barnsley, transplants to Northwest Georgia from England and Savannah, the estate was called Woodlands.

Although Barnsley had 100 servants, they were not slaves. He called them his Woodlands family. Barnsley desired to remain neutral during the Civil War, but his sons, George and Lucien, were ardent proponents of the Confederacy. In their support, he first donated $100,000 to the cause and allowed his merchant ships to act as blockade runners. Later, as the fortunes of the Confederacy plummeted, he sacrificed zinc from the estate's roof and iron from its pipes.

A Civil War skirmish occurred on the property on May 18, 1864. Barnsley and Confederate Col. R. G. Earle hid the women and children in the basements, the wine cellars, and the brandy room. But Mary Quinn—the Irish housekeeper—couldn't refrain from looking out at what she called "rogues and thieves." When Colonel Earle tried to protect her, he was killed. He is buried in the perennial bed just behind the ruins.

Not long afterward, Union Gen. James McPherson stayed at Woodlands, which he declared "one of the most beautiful spots on earth" and decreed that "no harm shall come to it as we are their guests." His admiration saved the estate from destruction.

However, after McPherson left, Union soldiers found $84,000 in Confederate bonds in Barnsley's safe and destroyed them in a bonfire into which Union soldiers tossed the contents of the house. After the war, Barnsley tried unsuccessfully to sue the U.S. government for $153,000 in damage and losses.

When Lucien Barnsley returned home after the war, it is documented that the first thing he saw was his sister, dirty and disheveled, coming from a meager garden clutching some vegetables. When he asked her why she was acting like a servant, she replied, "To survive, but God knows, not forever." Sound like a familiar scene?

Life didn't settle back to normal even then. George and Lucien Barnsley refused to sign an oath of allegiance to the Union. As a result, George left the country, emigrated to Brazil, and founded the town of Americana.

As you leave Barnsley Gardens, go back to State 140, turn right, and proceed to Adairsville. Of major strategic importance, the town contained large machine shops, a roundhouse, and a gun and powder factory. It was from the Adairsville Depot that Captain Fuller commandeered the *Texas* for the last leg of the Great Locomotive Chase.

During Sherman's March to the Sea, Confederate Gen. Joseph Johnston was unable to hold his position, and he split his forces to Kingston and Cassville, leaving Adairsville to be entered by Union troops, who destroyed part of the town. Although Adairsville is the only entire town in Georgia named to the National Register of Historic Places, most of the important homes and buildings are post–Civil War.

Pick up a "Guide to Historic Adairsville" at the 1902 Stock Exchange, 124 Public Square, where you can shop for antiques, books, and crafts, have a vintage portrait taken, or enjoy a gourmet lunch. Upstairs, the Public Square Opera House is a living-history dinner theater. Another popular restaurant is The Adairsville Inn, 100 South Main Street. The Great Locomotive Chase Festival is held annually in town the first week in October.

Continue south on US 41, then go west on State 293 to Kingston. Because of its location at the junction of the north-south and east-west railways, Kingston became the site of several hospitals and an ever-growing cemetery early in the war. General Sherman headquartered in Kingston on May 19–23, 1864, while his 90,000 men forded the Etowah River, which he dubbed "the Rubicon of Georgia." He returned after the fall of Atlanta to await General Grant's permission for the March to the Sea. Not quite a year later, on May 12, 1865, Kingston was the site of the last surrender of Confederates east of the Mississippi.

The Kingston Confederate Cemetery, on Johnson Street, contains the remains of 250 unknown Confederate dead and two Union dead. The cemetery was the site of the first Confederate Memorial Day celebration, called Decoration Day. Although the town was occupied by federal troops in the spring of 1864, the women of Kingston requested permission to decorate Confederate graves. The Union commandeer granted permission with the proviso that they decorate Union graves as well. Kingston is the only community in the nation to have an uninterrupted series of Memorial Day observances. A museum in the park is operated by the Kingston Women's History Club.

Retrace State 293 past US 41 to Cassville. Cultural center of North Georgia before the war, the thriving community contained two colleges, a splendid courthouse, four hotels, many shops, and fine homes. On May 19–20, 1864, General Johnston's rear guard of Confederate troops encountered Union troops near the Cassville Depot. The Confederates barricaded themselves inside and knocked out blocks for gun ports. A large section of the original structure remains. During the war, many Cassville homes were pressed into service as hospitals.

On November 5, 1864, citizens were given only twenty minutes' notice by invading Union troops before the town was burned. Although three churches and three houses survived, almost no documents or photographs were saved. Because the town was too far from the new railroad, it never recovered. Barely a blip on the landscape now, the town that once existed is identified only by a monument on what was the town square, a relief map describing the May 14, 1864, Battle of Cassville, and the Cassville Confederate Cemetery.

Located on a shady hillside on Cass White Road, the cemetery is the final resting place of 300 unknown Confederate soldiers. Native son Gen. William T. Wofford is buried there. He was one of three Cass County representatives who voted against seceding from the Union, but he went on to become Confederate commander in North Georgia and surrendered the last of the Southern troops at Kingston in 1865. In 1899, the Cassville chapter of the United Daughters of the Confederacy honored the dead by placing headstones at each of the unknown soldiers' graves. A large Confederate monument also praises them.

Go back to US 41 and turn south to Cartersville. Roselawn, at 224 West Cherokee Avenue, houses a collection of United Daughters of the Confederacy Civil War artifacts. The Bartow History Center, at 319 East Cherokee Avenue, traces the history of the county from the time that Native Americans were its only residents to the 1950s with uniforms, accessories, and personal articles, as well as extensive county records and genealogical information.

In an ironic footnote to history, Sherman had come to Bartow County as a tourist in 1848 to see the mysterious Etowah Indian Mounds (see Chieftans Trail). Later he joked, "I liked North Georgia so much, I came back and brought 100,000 of my closest friends." His intimate knowledge of the area was invaluable in planning his strategy for the Atlanta Campaign.

From US 41, take the exit for State 293 north. Instead of following State 293, immediately turn right onto Old Allatoona Road and go 1.5 miles. The Battle of Allatoona Pass, an indecisive battle to protect the railroad pass, occurred on October 5, 1864. With 3 million Union rations stored at the mouth of the pass, Sherman ordered his men to "Defend that place at all costs." Fifteen hundred casualties inspired the spiritual "Hold the Fort, For I am Coming."

The former roadbed is now an attractive, shaded hiking trail enclosed by steep-sided, tree-shrouded ridges capped by the remains of two forts. Adjacent to the pass entrance is the 1828 Clayton House, a private home, which served as a field hospital. Just down the road is the Grave of the Unknown Soldier. For many years, trains blew their whistles when they passed. Pillars remain visible of a bridge over the Etowah River that was burned by retreating Confederates.

Go back to US 41 and proceed south. Exit onto State 20 and go east. Almost immediately, you will turn right onto State 294, then follow the signs to the Visitors Center at Lake Allatoona. Located at a scenic overlook of Allatoona Dam, the center features Civil War relics and photographs. The thriving town of Etowah and Cooper's Iron Works, once at the base of the dam, supplied iron to the Confederacy. The town and foundries were destroyed by Union troops, but one cold-blast furnace survives. It, along with Mark Cooper's Friendship Monument and a fabulous view of the valley, can be seen from the overlook.

Go back to US 41, turn south on it until you get to State 92, and go west toward Dallas. New Hope Church Monument and Battle Site, off State 381, marks the spot where the federals were stopped on May 25, 1864, after ten days of battle. A relief map describes the conflicts.

Pickett's Mill State Historic Site, located on Mt. Tabor Road off Due West Road between State 381 and State 92, marks where the federals were stopped again on May 27, 1864, when their army of 14,000 troops attempted to outflank the Confederate position.

With only 10,000 troops, the Confederates decisively repulsed the federals—suffering only 500 losses to the federals' 1,600. Difficult terrain and a piecemeal attack contributed to the Union defeat.

The roads, ravines, and earthworks remain. Self-guided tours trace three loops that range in length from 1.1 to 1.7 miles. The visitors center has a museum and an audiovisual program. Monthly living-history programs on each third weekend demonstrate cooking, weapon firing, and military drill. The battle is reenacted annually. Guided nature tours are scheduled periodically.

A twenty-acre historical battlefield park off Due West Road marks the site of the Battle of Gilgal Church, which occurred on June 15–16, 1864. Although the church was destroyed and never rebuilt, eight acres of trenches are undisturbed.

Go back to US 41, turn east on State 293 to Kennesaw, then turn right on Cherokee Street. Located in an authentic cotton gin, the Big Shanty Museum in Kennesaw houses *The General*, the locomotive stolen by the Union from a spot only 100 yards away. *The General* survived the chase, and the Battle of Atlanta, and served throughout the war. Then cast aside, it sat in ruins, gradually being cloaked by kudzu, for several years. Fortunately, it was rescued, and restored; converted to coal and then oil, it has been used in expositions and centennials across the country. It was on display in Chattanooga before a legal battle brought it home to Kennesaw. The museum includes the locomotive and tender in a depotlike setting, descriptive exhibits, and an audiovisual presentation about its abduction. Located across the street is the old depot, which now houses art exhibits. Get a brochure from the museum for a walking tour of Kennesaw.

Retrace your steps on State 293, staying on it past US 41 to the Kennesaw Mountain National Battlefield Park, which commemorates the battles that occurred in June 1864 when Confederates successfully impeded Sherman's troops for three weeks. In fact, the Confederates holding the mountain were never defeated; Sherman finally made a flanking movement around them.

Located northwest of Marietta, the 2,800-acre park has a visitors center with a short audiovisual presentation and displays of artifacts, uniforms, and period photographs. Many challenging—though mostly paved—hiking trails ranging from two to fourteen miles crisscross the park. Eleven miles of earthworks remain. On a clear day, it's well worth the strenuous climb to the mountain crest to get the spectacular panorama of the Atlanta skyline and to see the memorial to fourteen Confederate generals who served there. If you're not up to the hike, on weekends there's a shuttle bus that will take you nearly to the top.

Several specific sites in the park deserve mention. At Kolb Farm, Daniel Butterfield, a Union commander, wrote "Taps." The "Dead Angle" at Cheatham Hill was the site of a huge federal attack foiled by the Confederates. The impressive Illinois Monument honors 480 men from that state who died here.

Staying on US 41 south, you'll come to Marietta, an important railroad town during the Civil War. Although the original Western & Atlantic Passenger Depot was destroyed by Sherman's troops, the replacement structure on Depot Street now houses the Marietta Welcome Center, where you can pick up brochures for two self-guided tours. The Cannonball Trail takes you past seventeen Civil War sites. The

Historic Marietta Walking-Driving Tour encompasses fifty-seven sites, including those on the Cannonball Trail.

Next door to the depot is Kennesaw House. Built in 1855 as a summer resort hotel called Fletcher House, it was the scene of a meeting between James Andrews and his Raiders the night before they stole *The General*. Sherman headquartered here on July 3, 1864. Partially burned when the federals pulled out of Marietta, the building was repaired and today houses a restaurant and offices.

Prior to the Civil War, Marietta was the home of the Georgia Military Institute, known as "The West Point of the South." In 1864, the entire cadet battalion joined the Confederate forces. During the Atlanta Campaign, 10,000 wounded soldiers were cared for in tents on the grounds. Federal troops burned the buildings in November 1864.

Several of the grand houses along Kennesaw Avenue suffered the humiliation of occupation by federal officers during the Atlanta Campaign. The First Presbyterian Church was used as a federal hospital. At St. James Episcopal Church, federals poured molasses into the pipe organ.

More than 3,000 soldiers from every state in the Confederacy, 1,000 of them unknown, are buried at the Marietta Confederate Cemetery, on Cemetery Street, including those killed in a train wreck at Allatoona Pass, those who died in Marietta hospitals, and bodies exhumed from Chickamauga and Atlanta and reburied here. Ten thousand Union soldiers are buried at the Marietta National Cemetery, at Washington Avenue and Cole Street, which continues to serve as an active national cemetery.

Marietta recovered from the war and continued to thrive after the turn of the century. It still retains an enchanting town square called Glover Park. During the Civil War, Confederate troops used it for muster and drill. Today lush landscaping, a fountain, gazebo, bandstand, and a miniature of

The General make the square among the prettiest in Georgia. Surrounding the square are the nationally known Theater on the Square, restaurants, and quaint shops such as The Brumby Chair Co., where artisans make rocking chairs, some of which are in the White House.

Radiating from the square are many blocks of stately Victorian mansions, several of which serve as bed and breakfasts: Sixty Polk Street; The Stanley House, at 236 Church Street; and Whitlock Inn, 57 Whitlock Avenue. Two well-known restaurants are Shillings on the Square and 1848 House—a gracious plantation house at 780 South Cobb Drive. Supposedly, the house was spared because of the owner's previous acquaintance with Sherman.

Take State 360 west out of Marietta and turn south on State 176 to reach Lithia Springs. With all the able-bodied men off to war, the women and children of Lithia Springs as well as Roswell were the only ones left to operate the textile mills supplying gray fabric to the Confederacy. During the Atlanta Campaign these women and children were rounded up by Union soldiers and deported north out of Georgia to prevent them from repairing the mills and resupplying the Confederate army. At least four hundred were abducted from Roswell by General Garrand. Never to be heard from again, their destiny remains a mystery. A fictionalized version of the fascinating story is told in *The Roswell Women*, by Frances Patton Statham.

Ruins of the Lithia Springs mill burned by Sherman's troops can be seen at Sweetwater Creek State Park.

Various ruins of the Roswell Mills remain at the Vickery Creek Unit of the Chattahoochee River National Recreation Area in Roswell. To get there, take State 120 east out of

Marietta to State 9 at the Town Square. The mills are just down over the hill.

When gold was discovered in the North Georgia mountains, the Bank of Darien—on Georgia's coast—sent Roswell King to open a branch in Auraria. He decided that the Chattahoochee River and two tributaries, Vickery Creek and Big Creek, at the foot of the Appalachian Mountains, would provide an abundant supply of waterpower for textile mills. King obtained land that had been wrested from the Cherokee. In 1838 he returned with a few other families to found a settlement later named after him. The flourishing textile mills he started provided the funds for building gracious homes and churches.

The mills of the Roswell Manufacturing Company were built between 1839 and 1864. It is from here that General Garrard's men abducted women and children before destroying the buildings. A machine shop, erected in 1853, is the only surviving structure. Roswell Mill itself was repaired after the war, but eventually the textile business died out in Roswell and the mills were closed in 1975. The buildings fell into disrepair and became almost completely engulfed by kudzu.

Several of the structures, however, have been resurrected for a new purpose. Shops, art galleries, restaurants, and nightspots give the buildings a new hum. An outdoor concert series is held in the courtyard throughout the summer.

King constructed two sets of row houses for millworkers. Called The Bricks, these houses on Sloan Street are thought to be among the first of their type in the country. Today, restored and serving as offices and a private club, they are occasionally open for tours.

Fortunately, when Roswell's mills were destroyed, few of the town's homes were damaged. Although most are privately owned, they are featured on walking and driving tours and are open periodically. You can get a brochure from the visitors center in the Old City Hall on the square, which is also the departure point for guided walking tours.

Roswell's most famous house is Bulloch Hall, 180 Bulloch Avenue. An 1840 Greek Revival mansion, it was the home of the Bulloch family, whose daughter Mittie was Theodore Roosevelt's mother and Eleanor Roosevelt's grandmother. Mittie was married in the house, and her son came for many visits, including one when he was president.

Today the house is owned by the city of Roswell and operated as a house museum, with a Civil War artifact room and Mittie's bedroom furnished as it was when she lived there. Costumed docents give scheduled tours, and several active guilds demonstrate quilting, basketry, candlemaking, open-hearth cooking, and other period skills.

Several festivals are held on the lawns each year, and the house also hosts changing art exhibits. During Christmas at Bulloch Hall—the highlight of the year—each room is furnished and embellished by an antique store or a decorator.

Flanking Bulloch Hall are Mimosa Hall, built in 1842, and Dolvin House. The late Victorian house is presently the home of an aunt of former president Jimmy Carter, who sometimes visits.

One of Roswell King's direct descendants, Miss Katherine Simpson, now in her nineties, still lives nearby in the 1842 Greek Revival Barrington Hall, named after Roswell King's son, Barrington King. Time had taken its toll on Barrington Hall until several volunteer groups stepped in and spruced it up. The house is sometimes open for tours.

Mimosa Boulevard displays a large concentration of antebellum homes as well as the historic Roswell Presbyterian Church. Built in 1840 as the first church in Roswell, it served as a federal hospital. Primrose Cottage, the first permanent home in Roswell, has an unusual hand-turned rosemary pine fence. Great Oaks, a brick residence built in 1842 for the first minister in town, later was headquarters for Union Gen. Kenner Garrard's cavalry troops.

Naylor Hall, built in 1840 on Canton Street, was the home of a mill supervisor. Ten-Fifty Canton Street is a charming bed and breakfast.

The Archibald Smith Plantation Home, 935 Alpharetta Highway/State 9, was built in 1845. The house and thirteen outbuildings stayed in the family for generations, preserved in their original state. The plantation accurately portrays the southern lifestyle of a prosperous mid-nineteenth-century cotton planter. A white oak tree on the property with a circumference of seventeen feet is thought to be the second largest in Georgia.

Commerce in Old Roswell was centered around the town square. Its historic buildings now house antique shops, boutiques, and The Public House—a well-known restaurant.

At the end of the nineteenth century, a new business district arose on Canton Street. Now called the Uptown Canton Street Historic District, this area of Victorian-era buildings houses boutiques, antique shops, several art galleries, and Gabe's Lodge, a popular Italian restaurant. Our favorite Roswell restaurant is Lickskillet Farm, 1380 Old Roswell Road, located in a restored farmhouse tucked away outside of town in a pastoral setting.

Our next stop is Atlanta. Avoid a lot of congestion and traffic lights by taking State 400 south from Roswell to Atlanta.

The fall of Atlanta in September 1864 was a turning point in the war and sealed the fate of the Confederacy. Although "that pyromaniac from the North," as Sherman is uncharitably known in the South, instituted massive destruction in Georgia, he really isn't responsible for the burning of Atlanta. In trying to blow up ammunition left there, fleeing Confederates actually sparked the fire.

From his victory in Atlanta, Sherman returned to Kingston, from which he had begun his infamous march across the state to Savannah—capturing Savannah by Christmas that year. His troops then turned north, exiting Georgia at Augusta.

Many of the significant battle positions around Atlanta are little more than historical markers—the sites themselves obliterated by urbanization. However, the impressive new Atlanta History Museum at the Atlanta History Center, 130 West Paces Ferry Road in Buckhead, features a Civil War exhibit called "Gone for a Soldier," dedicated to the everyday experiences of typical soldiers both North and South. This is the largest display of Civil War artifacts in the Southeast. Pick up the replicas of a knapsack and a rifle—you'll be astounded at the weight the common foot soldier carried every day. Each July, the history center sponsors a weekend reenactment.

Don't miss the Cyclorama in Grant Park, off Boulevard south of I-20. The 100-year-old, 400- by 50-foot circular painting depicts the Battle of Atlanta. Transport yourself to a hot day in September 1864, when guns crashed and smoke and screams filled the air. Theater-style seating revolves as music, narration, lighting, sound effects, and a three-dimensional diorama recreate that fateful battle. Atlanta's beautifully restored painting is one of only twenty remaining worldwide. The *Texas*, the locomotive that eventually overtook *The General*, is displayed in the lobby.

In 1864, Father Thomas O'Reilly of the Shrine of the Immaculate Conception, 48 Martin Luther King Drive, S. W., sent a message to Union soldiers. "If you burn the Catholic Church, all Catholics in the ranks of the Union Army will mutiny." He also asked that other churches, City Hall, and the courthouse be spared. His request was granted.

Many visitors think that everything they need to know about the Civil War can be learned from *Gone With the Wind*, opus of Atlanta's own Margaret Mitchell. Although that is a misconception, the book and movie have played a major role in Georgia and Atlanta's tourism industry. Recently opened at 659 Peachtree Street, the Road to Tara Museum exhibits one of the world's largest displays of *Gone With the Wind* memorabilia.

Historic Oakland Cemetery, 248 Oakland Avenue in downtown Atlanta, is Margaret Mitchell Marsh's final resting place. The grave marker is so simple, it's easy to miss. In the Confederate section of the cemetery, 2,500 Confederate soldiers, including 5 generals, and 20 Union soldiers are buried. The great Confederate Lion marks a section of unknown dead. The lion was carved from a 30,000-pound block of Kennesaw marble from Tate, Georgia, at that time the largest block ever quarried. When the sixty-five-foot Confederate Obelisk was unveiled in 1874, it was the tallest structure in Atlanta.

In addition to Atlanta's myriad hotels, there are several bed and breakfasts in the area, including Shellmont, 821 Piedmont Avenue; Woodruff, 223 Ponce de Leon Avenue; Ansley Inn, 253 Fifteenth Street; Heartfield Manor, 182 Elizabeth Street; and Oakwood House, 951 Edgewood Avenue. Good restaurants in every price range are too numerous to mention.

Although it is not on the Blue and Gray Trail, you should visit Stone Mountain, east of downtown on US 78 or State 124. On the face of this mountain—one of the largest granite outcroppings in the world—is carved a gigantic bas relief memorial depicting mounted Confederate heroes President Jefferson Davis, Gen. Robert E. Lee, and Gen. Stonewall Jackson. During the ever-popular finale of the nightly summer laser shows, the horses and men come to life and circle the mountain to the strains of "Dixie." No matter how many times you've seen it, you'll get goose bumps. Also within the park grounds are a Civil War Museum and an Antebellum

Plantation, created by moving buildings from other parts of Georgia.

Visitors often search fruitlessly for Tara, only to learn that the plantation existed solely in Mitchell's imagination. However, in Jonesboro, just south of Atlanta, you can tour 1879 Ashley Oaks, 144 College Street, and 1839 Stately Oaks, 100 Carriage Lane, thought to have been among the homes that inspired Mitchell's Tara and Ashley Wilkes's Twelve Oaks (see the Peach Blossom Trail).

Few parts of Georgia were spared action during the Civil War. For more Civil War attractions, see particularly the chapters on the Antebellum Trail, Andersonville Trail, Coastin' Along Georgia's Seaboard, Golden Isles, and the Peach Blossom Trail. However, there are Civil War sites mentioned in every chapter.

In addition to its Civil War locations, Northwest Georgia offers a cornucopia of other attractions. Because the Chieftans Trail and Blue and Gray Trail are both located in the Northwest Georgia mountains, the two trails are near many of the same attractions. See the Chieftans Trail for further information.

In the Area

Barnsley Gardens, 597 Barnsley Gardens Road, Adairsville, GA 30103, 404-773-7480.

Bartow History Center, 319 East Cherokee Avenue, P.O. Box 1239, Cartersville, GA 30120, 404-382-3818.

Big Shanty Museum, 2829 Cherokee Street, Kennesaw, GA 30144, 404-427-2117.

51

Cartersville-Bartow County Tourism Council, P.O. Box 200397, Cartersville, GA 30120, 404-387-1357.

Catoosa County Chamber of Commerce, P.O. Box 52, Ringgold, GA 30736, 706-965-5201.

Chattanooga Area Convention and Visitors Bureau, 1001 Market Street, P.O. Box 1111, Chattanooga, TN 37401, 800-322-3344.

Chickamauga Chamber of Commerce, c/o Gordon Lee Mansion, 217 Cove Street, Chickamauga, GA 30707, 706-374-4728.

Chickamauga-Chattanooga National Military Park, P.O. Box 2128, Fort Oglethorpe, GA 30742, 706-866-9241.

Clisbe Austin House, The Tunnel Hill Historical Foundation, P.O. Box 114, Tunnel Hill, GA 30755, 706-673-5152.

Dalton Convention and Visitors Bureau, 524 Holiday Avenue, Dalton, GA 30720, 706-278-7373.

Douglas County Welcome Center, P.O. Box 395, Douglasville, GA 30133, 404-942-5022.

Fannin County Chamber of Commerce, P.O. Box 875, Blue Ridge, GA 30513, 706-632-5680.

Gordon County Chamber of Commerce and Welcome Center, 300 South Wall Street, Calhoun, GA 30701, 706-625-3200.

Greater Rome Convention and Visitors Bureau, P.O. Box 5323, Rome, GA 30161, 706-295-5576.

Marietta Welcome Center, 4 Depot Street, Marietta, GA 30060, 404-429-1115.

Northwest Georgia Travel Association, P.O. Box 184, Calhoun, GA 30703-0184, 706-629-3406.

Paulding County Chamber of Commerce, 150 East Memorial Drive, Dallas, GA 30132, 404-445-6016.

Pickett's Mill Historic Site, 2640 Mt. Tabor Road, Dallas, GA 30132, 404-443-7850.

Historic Roswell Convention and Visitors Bureau, 617 Atlanta Street, Roswell, GA 30075, 404-640-3253.

Tunnel Hill Historical Foundation, P.O. Box 114, Tunnel Hill, GA 30755, 706-673-5152.

4 ~

Chattahoochee Trace

Getting there: Take US 27 or US 29 to where they intersect at La Grange.

Highlights: *Pine Mountain's Callaway Gardens resort, historic districts of Columbus, the National Infantry Museum, living history in Westville, Fort Gaines Frontier Village, and Indian mounds.*

The mighty Chattahoochee River's headwaters begin with an unassuming trickle in the wild mountains of Northeast Georgia, then grow in strength to course on a southwesterly route that sometimes tumbles over rocks or plunges over abrupt promontories. Periodically, the river's route is interrupted to create lakes and generate electric power as well as to provide drinking water for the towns and cities along its path. By the time the Chattahoochee reaches Atlanta, it's so exhausted and meandering that you cross it again and again. Then the river picks up new vigor as it flows into West Point Lake near La Grange, then forms the border between Georgia and Alabama as it continues to flow south to the Florida panhandle. At the peak of its vitality, the Chattahoochee is navigable from Columbus south.

Most rivers used to create political boundaries are divided in the middle, but the Chattahoochee belongs entirely to Georgia. The boundary is on the Alabama shore, resulting in plenty of official wrangling between the neighbor states.

Although Georgians and Alabamians may disagree about the ownership and usage of the waters in the Chattahoochee River, both states have formed a unique partnership to champion the scenic, historic, and recreational attractions on both banks of the river. The Historic Chattahoochee Commission (HCC) unites eighteen counties in the two states—eleven of them in Georgia— into the Chattahoochee Trace, stretching from La Grange, Georgia, to the Florida border.

Founded in 1970, the HCC is the first and only tourism/ preservation agency in the nation with authority to cross state lines in pursuing goals common to all of the counties involved.

A pleasurable mixture of romantic Old South heritage and New South innovations, the area is a mecca for every type of vacationer—history buff, camper, environmentalist, birdwatcher, hunter, fisherman, cyclist, and bed and breakfast aficionado. The region is rich in lakes, championship golf courses, historic structures, and Native American sites, as well as phenomenal natural topography. Pilgrimages and festivals abound.

In this book, we've recounted the attractions on the Georgia side of the river, but keep in mind that there are just as many on the Alabama side (described in *Country Roads of Alabama*, Country Roads Press, 1995). We'd suggest at least a long weekend to explore the Georgia side.

Beginning at the northern end of the trail, at the intersection of US 27 and US 29, is La Grange, a lovely, small city with a variety of attractions. At the Troup County Historical Society, 136 Main Street, you'll find a library of local history and genealogy. The society sponsors periodic tours of some of the town's finest homes, including Bellevue, 204 Ben Hill Street, the 1854 Greek Revival home of statesman Benjamin Harvey Hill, who entertained notables such as Jefferson Davis. Hill was later arrested for this offense by Union soldiers.

The Callaway Memorial Tower, Truitt and Fourth Avenues, built in 1929 to salute textile magnate Fuller E. Callaway, Sr., was patterned after the Campanile of St. Mark's Square in Venice, Italy. The LaFayette Fountain, located in LaFayette Square, salutes Revolutionary War hero Marquis de LaFayette, after whose French estate La Grange was named. The statue is a replica of the one in LePuy, France.

Art lovers will enjoy the Chattahoochee Valley Art Association, located in the renovated 1892 Troup County Jail, at 112 Hines Street. The galleries feature changing exhibits, and the shop offers the work of regional artisans.

La Grange College—Georgia's oldest independent school—was mentioned in *Gone With the Wind*. On the campus is the Lamar Dodd Art Center, which features changing exhibits, a permanent collection, and retrospective works by Dodd—one of Georgia's most noted artists—as well as the Southwest and Plains American Indian collection.

Stop by for a delicious lunch served in elegant surroundings at In Clover, 205 Broad Street. You can pick up a brochure for the National Register of Historic Places Driving Tour of Troup County—a self-guided tour of thirteen sites of antebellum, Greek Revival, and plantation styles—from the Troup County Archives, at 136 Main Street, or from the Troup County Chamber of Commerce, at 224 Main Street.

Continue west on State 109 to one of the Southeast's premier fishing spots—West Point Lake. The 25,900-acre lake boasts some of the best crappie and largemouth and hybrid bass fishing in Georgia. Recreational facilities include two commercial marinas, four beaches, six major camping areas, and a 10,000-acre wildlife management area. You'll also want to explore the West Point Dam Visitors Center and Power-house Exhibit.

In the town of West Point, south of La Grange on US 29, a historical marker at West Tenth Street and Sixth Avenue identifies Fort Tyler, the scene of one of the last skirmishes of the Civil War. There's a Confederate cemetery off US 29 at East Eleventh Street. Drive around West Point to admire the varied architecture.

Go east on State 18 to Pine Mountain, home of Callaway Gardens, a diverse and unique resort that is familiar to and beloved by Georgians. For a day's excursion, business confer-ence, family vacation, or sports interlude, Callaway's facili-ties and services meet every mood and need. The 2,500-acre horticultural display garden and 14,000-acre resort are open year-round.

Callaway's focal point is the 12,000 acres of woodlands, lakes, and gardens. But what other garden can you name that offers an inn with a variety of fine dining experiences, cot-tages, villas, a lodge, golf, tennis, trap, skeet, quail hunting, sailing, bass and bream fishing, swimming, water-ski spec-taculars, a summer recreation program, and the Florida State University's "Flying High Circus"? Thirteen lakes and more than twenty miles of roadways and hiking and bicycling trails open the woodland and garden areas to visitors.

Conceived by textile magnate Cason J. Callaway, Sr., the resort began in the thirties as a humble vacation retreat. Callaway's experimentation with reclaiming wasted cotton fields led to an ever-growing garden. Opened to the public in 1952, the resort includes trails dedicated to azaleas, wildflow-ers, and rhododendron, as well as the world's largest public display of hollies—more than 450 species. Of the 700 varieties of azaleas, the most important is the orange plumleaf, or prunifolia—a summer bloomer that grows natively only in the vicinity of Pine Mountain.

Mr. Cason's Vegetable Garden includes a section used for the set of the PBS series *Victory Garden South*. Another area is devoted to flowers and plants that attract butterflies.

The John A. Sibley Horticultural Center is an outstanding conservatory. Rather than just a gigantic glass greenhouse, this is an environment where the indoors and outdoors blend almost imperceptibly. Featuring temperate and tropical plants and containing a two-story waterfall, the center presents eighteen major floral displays annually as well as a changing topiary exhibit.

Opened in 1988, the Cecil B. Day Butterfly Center is the largest glass-enclosed tropical butterfly garden in North America. More than 1,000 "flowers of the air" soar freely as visitors stroll among them. Some of these bursts of living color may even light on you. In addition to a constantly moving garden of rich hues, this paradise regained also hosts tropical plants, hummingbirds, mandarin ducks, bleeding heart doves, and other ground birds. G. Harold Northrop, former president of Callaway, called it "the most significant environmental project, in terms of helping people understand the delicate balance of nature, that has been started in this country."

For those to whom Christmas isn't Christmas without snow, your best chance of actually encountering a hassle-free blizzard in Georgia is by touring Callaway Gardens' Christmas extravaganza—"Fantasy in Lights." In addition to snowflakes, visions of sugarplums will dance in front of your eyes as you encounter them—in living color and more than life-size—on the five-mile, audiovisual ride-through that lasts from Thanksgiving weekend through New Year's Day. The after-dark attraction claims to be the largest outdoor lighted exhibition in the nation.

Cason Callaway once said, "Every child ought to see something beautiful before he's six years old—something he will remember all his life." Mr. Callaway could never have envisioned the enchanted winter festival that has been added to his garden, but no matter what time of year, Callaway Gardens has provided that first glimpse of splendor to a continual procession of children of all ages.

Other highlights of the resort include the English Gothic Ida Cason Callaway Memorial Chapel, constructed of Georgia materials, and a pioneer log cabin where living history is presented periodically.

Another glamorous annual event, which we always try to attend, is the Callaway Steeplechase, held each November for the benefit of community arts groups. On a crisp fall afternoon, enthusiasts gather for one of the most beautiful hunt meets in the nation. Sharp turns, steep inclines, and numerous jumps provide an element of danger that's exciting enough for anyone. The premier event is the Sport of Kings Challenge, one horse race in a series that goes on to England and Wales. Food is an important element of the festivities, whether it's a private feast in an elaborately decorated tent, a casual tailgate repast, or the Taste of the Chase—a sampling from different restaurants. Callaway Gardens offers a weekend package that includes accommodations and a Harvest Festival of Wine and Food.

In the historic village of Pine Mountain, you'll find more than fifty gift and antique shops and restaurants. Historical records, photos, and local artifacts are displayed at Chipley Historical Center, McDougald Avenue.

The Storms House, 207 Harris Street, is a glorious Victorian bed and breakfast. Comfortable accommodations can be found just south of Pine Mountain in Hamilton's Wedgwood Inn and the rustic Annie's Log Cabin—big enough for an entire family.

Two miles north of Pine Mountain, at 1300 Oak Grove Road, is the Pine Mountain Wild Animal Park—500 acres with 200 to 300 animals wandering freely. You can take a self-guided driving tour or a guided bus tour. Other attractions include an authentic farm operation, serpentarium, monkey house, petting zoo, and gift shop.

Between Pine Mountain and Warm Springs on State 190 are Franklin D. Roosevelt State Park and the twenty-seven-mile Pine Mountain Trail. Originally developed by the Civilian Conservation Corps, the park covers 10,000 acres and offers thirty miles of hiking trails, waterfalls, beaver dams, ponds, and a rocky overlook called Buzzard's Roost. In addition, the park has cabins, RV campsites, a scenic drive, picnicking, and fishing. A special treat at the park is the Roosevelt Riding Stables, on State 354, where you can take guided trail rides that last anywhere from an hour to five days with overnight camping.

The village of Warm Springs grew between 1881 and 1907 when it was discovered that the natural spring waters had rehabilitative powers for polio therapy. Franklin D. Roosevelt was one of those who sought relief. He came so often, he built a house there in 1932. In fact, it is the only house he ever owned.

Now the Little White House Historic Site, on State 85 west, the president's house has been left exactly as it was the day he died in 1945. Also on the grounds is a museum of memorabilia tracing Roosevelt's life.

Locals tell stories of the president pulling up outside the drugstore of the Hotel Warm Springs in a chauffeur-driven convertible to buy a Coca-Cola and chat with townsfolk.

Something died in Warm Springs when Roosevelt passed away. The town and hotel went into a drastic decline. Today the revitalized village houses several restaurants and sixty-five shops purveying souvenirs, crafts, antiques, and furniture. Superb bed and breakfast accommodations are available at the Hotel Warm Springs, 17 Broad Street. This was where visiting dignitaries, secret service agents, and media representatives stayed when FDR was at the Little White House. Rescued from oblivion and restored to its 1941 appearance, the hotel contains a restaurant, an old-fashioned ice-cream parlor, and several craft shops.

You can either retrace State 190 to Pine Mountain and turn south on US 27, or you can take State 85 west to US 27 Alternate to Columbus.

Columbus is a treasure trove of architectural gems. Numerous structures and entire districts are included in the National Register of Historic Places or are National Historic Landmarks.

The center of the Sunbelt South has several other nicknames—Fountain City, inspired by its numerous fountains; Port City, because it is the northernmost navigable port on the Chattahoochee River; Soft Drink Capital, because the Coca-Cola, Royal Crown, and Nehi formulas were devised by local residents; and Georgia's West Coast, because the city borders Alabama not only with the Chattahoochee but with several man-made lakes.

Begin with Heritage Corner, a walking tour of five historic 1820s to 1870s properties at Seventh Street and Broadway. One of the dwellings—a two-story Second Empire Victorian at 700 Broadway—houses the Historic Columbus Foundation, where you can get tour tickets. The Victorian cottage at 11 Seventh Street is the former home of John Stith Pemberton, originator of the Coca-Cola formula. It might surprise you to learn that he made only $1,500 on his concoction. Part of his property includes an old kitchen house and apothecary shop. The Walker-Peters-Langdon House, at

716 Broadway, is an 1828 Federal cottage with period furnishings. Also on the grounds is an 1800s log cabin and an 1840 farmhouse that serves as the gift shop.

Get a brochure for Original City Tours from the Convention and Visitors Bureau at 801 Front Street. The tour is divided into three parts. Uptown includes the restored Victorian Springer Opera House, 103 Tenth Street. The State Theater of Georgia, Edwin Booth, Oscar Wilde, John Philip Sousa, Will Rogers, and Irving Berlin played there. Try to attend a play if you can; the season runs from September through May.

High Uptown includes many opulent residences, such as the Rankin House, 1440 Second Avenue, which boasts the finest ironwork in Columbus. The historic district encompasses Heritage Corner, the Chattahoochee Promenade along the river, the Columbus Ironworks Convention and Trade Center, the Confederate Naval Museum, and such houses as the Folly, at 527 First Avenue, the nation's only antebellum double-octagonal house.

The James W. Woodruff, Jr., Confederate Naval Museum—the only Confederate naval museum—contains the remains of the ironclad ram *Muscogee* and the gunboat *Chattahoochee*, as well as prototypes of experimental vessels, other Confederate artifacts, weapons, and models.

The Ironworks was a major producer of cast-iron products, agricultural implements, industrial and building supplies, and steam engines. During the Civil War, it was a major supplier of cannons and iron cladding and engines for Confederate gunboats and rams. After the war, it settled down to making ice machines until 1965. The abandoned building was rehabilitated into a convention facility.

The Columbus Museum, located at 1251 Wynnton Road, is the second-largest art museum in the state. Renowned for its permanent and changing fine art exhibitions, it also offers a film, *The Chattahoochee Legacy*, a regional history gallery, and an interactive youth museum.

Columbus also contains a wealth of landmarks connected with Black history. A brochure is available for a driving tour from the Convention and Visitors Bureau. The tour of twenty-four sites includes churches, cemeteries, a theater, businesses, and the homes of prominent Black residents such as famous jazz singer Ma Rainey and the first Black combat pilot, Eugene Bullard.

A busy, commercial city, Columbus is the home of several manufacturing or production plants, which you can tour—*Columbus Ledger-Enquirer* newspaper; Dolley Madison snack cakes; Kinnett Dairies; Sunshine Biscuits; Swift Textiles—one of the top U.S. producers of denim—and Tom's Foods, makers of candy, snacks, cookies, and crackers.

Columbus is noted for several specialty dishes—the Country Captain, a tomato and chicken dish, and the Scramble Dog—and the tradition of putting peanuts in your Coca-Cola. Don't leave Columbus without eating at the Goetchius House, 405 Broadway, also located in the historic district. Magnificent Continental cuisine is served in the 1839 New Orleans–style mansion furnished with Victorian and Empire antiques.

South of Columbus on US 27/US 280 is Fort Benning, home of the U.S. Army's Infantry School, where you can tour the National Infantry Museum—one of the largest and most complete collections of military and small arms in the country. The Hall of the U.S. Infantry traces the evolution of the infantry from the French and Indian War to the present. The Hall of Flags displays military art and military documents signed by all U.S. presidents, silver presentation pieces, weapons, and an exhibit honoring Gen. Omar Bradley, who served at Fort Benning. Captured military paraphernalia is displayed in the Axis Powers Exhibit.

At Cusseta, turn south on US 27/State 1 and follow it to Lumpkin, where you can take the Old Stagecoach Trail for a driving tour of historic homes. Get a brochure from the 1836 Bedingfield Inn. Located on the town square, the inn was once a stagecoach stop and is now a museum. Private rooms were available for overnight guests, or they could sleep several to a bed in the unheated Common Room. The Hatchett Drug Store—also on the square—recreates a turn-of-the-century apothecary shop with an outstanding collection of artifacts. Take time to view the imposing courthouse and the wonderful general store.

Make sure you have plenty of color film, then take State 39C west to Georgia's "Little Grand Canyon," Providence Canyon State Conservation Park. Coming as a complete surprise to the visitor, the 150-foot-deep canyon is the result of only 100 years of soil erosion. The varicolored ravine walls produce a beautiful natural painting. In addition to spectacular panoramas, the park has the highest concentration of wildflowers in the state and many plumleaf azaleas—found only in the Presidential Pathways region. The park includes an interpretive center, picnic areas, hiking and backpacking trails, pioneer camps, and a group shelter.

Visit Florence Marina State Park, located on State 39C on Lake Walter F. George. In addition to water sports and hiking/nature trails, the park has the Kirby Interpretive Center, which explains the rich history of Stewart County through displays of artifacts from the prehistoric Paleo-Indian period through the present. Eight Rood Creek Indian Mounds from the period of A.D. 900 to 1540 can be explored only on a guided tour. Five of the mounds are situated around what was a central plaza and range in size from three-foot circular mounds to twenty-five-foot pentagonal pyramids. Surrounded by moats, this was the largest Native American settlement in the Chattahoochee River Basin.

Go back to Lumpkin and turn south on US 27. Just a few miles out of town is Westville—"where it's always 1850." This working village of relocated, authentically restored original mid-nineteenth-century buildings is populated with costumed guides who provide living history and demonstrations. By restoring and relocating original buildings, a village has been created that realistically depicts Georgia's preindustrial life and the culture of the 1850s. If you're lucky, you'll be there when the enticing aroma of baking gingerbread will lead you to try a sample. Authentic handicrafts and other gifts are available at the Country Store.

Annual events include the Fair of 1850, held during the last week in October and the first week in November. Demonstrations of harvest-time activities such as cane grinding and syrup making take place, and the last remaining antebellum animal-powered cotton gin operates. During December, period decorations and festivities celebrate the season.

Continue south on US 27 to Cuthbert. Home of Andrew College—second college in the country to grant degrees to women—the small town also had two other colleges. Pick up a brochure at the Chamber of Commerce on Court Street for a self-guided historic tour that includes thirty-four antebellum to Victorian homes, the courthouse, depot, and college. Practically every home on College Street is an architectural masterpiece. The McWilliams-Harris House, 918 College Street, was so perfectly proportioned that it was used as a model for Franklin D. Roosevelt's Little White House in Warm Springs. The King-Stapleton House, 712 College Street, is an outstanding example of Greek Revival architecture.

The simpler Fletcher Henderson House, on Andrews Street, was the home of a leading Black educator and his son, famous musician Fletcher Henderson, Jr., who was credited with being the single most important figure in the development of Big Band jazz. Henderson, Jr., is buried in

Greenwood Cemetery on Hamilton Street, as are other notable citizens and Confederate soldiers who died at the college when it served as a hospital.

The Freight Depot, 216 Front Street, was built in 1860 from limestone and is the only one of its kind in Georgia. Cuthbert has more porticoed Greek Revival business offices than any town in Georgia. Of particular interest are those on Court Street, which served as law and medical offices when they were built in the 1880s and continue to do so today.

As you continue south on US 27, take a short detour west on State 37 to Fort Gaines. In this unusual area, mountain laurel indigenous to North Georgia coexists with maidenhair fern native to Florida. Cemocheechobee Creek meanders about the area. The name of the creek is quite fitting—it means "a blind horse staggering through the woods." An Indian mound dates to A.D. 300, and remnants exist of an Indian village dating to A.D. 700.

You've probably heard the phrase "We'll be there if the good Lord's willing and the creek don't rise." The creek being referred to isn't a stream, but rather the Creek Indians at the time of the American Revolution.

Explore Fort Gaines Frontier Village, a partial replica of a frontier fort established in 1814. It became a fort against Indian attacks in 1836, then served as a Confederate fort in 1863. Its purpose was to prevent Union troops from getting up the Chattahoochee River to Columbus—a vital shipbuilding city with an ironworks and textile plants. Grist- and cane mills and log cabins are exhibited. The Otus Micco statue—a handcrafted eighteen-foot-tall Indian totem—overlooks the Chattahoochee River. It is the only memorial to a Creek Indian that is actually in the old Creek Nation.

An interesting story is told about the period following the War of 1812. A boat containing settlers was attacked by Indians. Only two men escaped and a woman was captured.

During her captivity, when the Indians raided a cabin or set-tlement, they would throw away any paper money they found. She gathered it up and pinned it to her petticoats with thorns or pine needles. Later when she was freed, she and her new husband, John Dill, used the money to build the magnif-icent Dill House, now being restored.

Between the War of 1812 and the Civil War, Fort Gaines was a prosperous steamboat town. Several houses of that period are of historical or architectural significance. McRae House served as a Confederate hospital, and McAlister House as a prison for Union soldiers. The Toll House is from the 1820s, when the only way across the Chattahoochee was by ferry.

Today Fort Gaines is a tranquil village actively looking for people who'd like to retire there. We love the town's slogan: "We will accept characters, but not malcontents. We aspire to be the best small town in Georgia."

While near Fort Gaines, check out the Walter F. George Lock and Dam, the second-highest lock lift east of the Missis-sippi. The lake has more than 640 miles of shoreline and twenty-three public access areas. George Bagby State Park, on the lake, has motel and camping facilities.

You can take State 39 south and visit the Outpost Replica, a reconstructed fort, circa 1816–30, used to protect settlers from Creek and Seminole Indian attacks.

Proceed on State 39 to Blakely to see the Kolomoki Mounds State Historic Park. The park features a temple mound—one of the largest east of the Mississippi—and an interpretive center, which allows access into a partially exca-vated mound.

In Blakely, you'll want to take a picture of the peanut monument on Courthouse Square. Also on the square is the last wooden Confederate flagpole, erected in 1861. West of the city, off State 62 and Old River Road, is the Coheelee

Creek Covered Bridge. It is two spans wide and ninety-two feet long. On the Chattahoochee River is Lake George Andrews, which offers water sports, camping, and picnicking.

The southern area of the Trace is known as the wiregrass region, because the native grass is noted for its tough, wiry roots. In the extreme south, the Chattahoochee and Flint Rivers meet and flow into man-made Lake Seminole, a 37,500-acre lake. Seminole State Park offers camping, cottages, a beach, fishing, and water sports. You've now reached the Georgia/Florida border and the end of the Chattahoochee Trace.

If you're interested in exploring all or part of the Chattahoochee Trace, we highly recommend the brochure "Chattahoochee Trace: Mini-Tour Guide." It organizes tours based on interests such as architecture or historic landmarks, and includes maps, visitor information and welcome center locations, bed and breakfasts, historic restaurants, marinas and boating facilities, U.S. Army Corps of Engineers public use areas, National Register of Historic Places and National Historic Landmark structures, hunting lodges, and a calendar of events. The guide is invaluable in providing information on days and hours of operation, current admission information, and directions to the attractions. It is available from the Historic Chattahoochee Commission.

A trip down this river corridor is an exciting and educational experience—a journey through the ages that will make you realize that there's no time like the present for savoring the many attractions of the Trace.

In the Area

Callaway Gardens Resort, Pine Mountain, GA 31822-2000,
    800-282-8181.

Chattahoochee Trace, 136 Main Street, La Grange, GA 30241, 706-845-8440.

Cuthbert-Randolph County Chamber of Commerce, Court Street, Cuthbert, GA 31740, 912-732-2683.

Fort Gaines-Clay County Visitors Bureau, Route 1, Box 239A, Fort Gaines, GA 31751, 912-768-3195.

Georgia Visitors Information Center, I-85 at Williams Road, Columbus, GA 31904, 706-649-7455.

Georgia Visitors Information Center, I-85, West Point, GA 31833, 706-645-3353.

Historic Chattahoochee Commission at P.O. Box 33, Eufaula, AL 36072-0033, 205-687-9755.

Meriwether County Chamber of Commerce, P.O. Box 9, Warm Springs, GA 31830, 706-655-2558.

Pine Mountain Tourism Association, P.O. Box 177, Pine Mountain, GA 31822, 706-663-4000.

Pine Mountain Welcome Center, 101 Broad Street, Pine Mountain, GA 31822, 800-441-3502.

Roosevelt Riding Stables, State 354, Pine Mountain, GA 31822, 706-628-4533.

Troup County Chamber of Commerce, 224 Main Street, La Grange, GA 30240, 706-884-8671.

5 ~

Chieftains Trail

Highlights: *Native American history, Indian mounds, Chieftains Museum, and the Chief Vann House—showpiece of the Cherokee Nation.*

They were plantation owners—some were slaveholders— and they built some of Georgia's first white-columned mansions. They were of part Scotch and Irish descent with names such as Ross, Vann, Ridge, and McIntosh. They were college educated and traveled abroad. No, these were not the white elite of Georgia. They were Creek and Cherokee Indian chiefs of Northwest Georgia. Their advanced culture defied the traditional view of Indian life.

Today each of their homesteads is a featured site on the Chieftains Trail, a 150-mile route through what the Cherokees called "The Enchanted Land." The trail connects nine prominent attractions tracing the region's Native American history from ancient times to the infamous Trail of Tears in 1837–38.

Here you will find vestiges of three separate and distinct Native American cultures: the prehistoric Mississippian culture, the Creek Nation, and the Cherokee Nation. Created by the Georgia legislature in 1988 to commemorate the 150th anniversary of the Trail of Tears, the Chieftains Trail stretches through West Georgia from the Georgia/Tennessee border to Carrollton, south of I-20, with an eastern loop to Chatsworth and Tate.

Vast mineral wealth was locked beneath the Georgia mountains. Native Americans used these bounties from nature in their everyday existence. The Mississippian culture, which extended from Wisconsin and Minnesota south to Georgia and west to the Great Plains, thrived from A.D. 800 to the advent of the first European explorers. In 1540 Hernando de Soto led 650 Spanish soldiers, businessmen, entrepreneurs, and priests through the region searching for gold, often taking shelter with Native Americans and visiting the Etowah Indian settlements.

These ancient people of the Mississippian culture had a sophisticated trading structure, were skilled craftsmen, and practiced advanced religious customs. Their towns were located in river basins where they fished and cultivated crops. Natives decorated themselves with shell beads, tattoos, paint, complicated hairdos, feathers, and copper ear ornaments.

Chief priests, who commanded fortified villages, lived in temples atop enormous earthen mounds overlooking the towns. Upon the chief's death, he was buried in the mound, his temple was demolished, and another layer of earth was added to the mound for his successor. Nobility were buried in elaborate costumes accompanied by items they would need in their afterlives. The Mississippian Culture declined, however, partly due to the spread of European diseases as well as wars with the intruders.

In more modern times, but prior to the early eighteenth century, the predominant Native American group in Georgia and Alabama belonged to the Creek Confederacy. Today's Creek Nation, also known as the Muskogee, was the major tribe.

Most of the groups of the confederacy, who migrated from the Southwest, shared language, ceremonies, and village layout. Large permanent towns similar to the arrangements of the Mississippian people were centered around plazas used for religious ceremonies, dancing, and games. The plazas contained a rotunda—a round building used for council meetings—and an open-air summer council house. Towns were governed by a chief and an assistant chief.

The Creek Nation occupied the Etowah Valley territory near Cartersville until the late 1700s. Although the Creek and Cherokee had lived peacefully as neighbors, a great war occurred in the late 1700s that resulted in the retreat of the Creek Nation to south of the Chattahoochee River. That site will be described later.

The Cherokee Nation was the largest of the five civilized tribes of the Southeast, which also included Choctaws, Chickasaws, Seminoles, and Creeks. The Cherokees are of Iroquoian lineage and migrated to the southern Appalachians from the Great Lakes region. They called their new home "Chiaha"—the meeting of the hills and the waters. The Cherokee were agrarian people who lived in log homes. By 1650, the Nation was a confederacy of towns that controlled more than 40,000 square miles with a population of 22,500.

Their only period of combat with whites was during the American Revolution when the Cherokees, Creeks, and Choctaw supported the British. As a result of being on the wrong side, the tribal holdings of Native Americans were substantially diminished.

After 1800, the Cherokees abandoned the traditional tribal system and adopted many aspects of white culture—their form of government and style of dress, as well as farming and home-building methods. Many Cherokee women married white settlers.

Sequoyah (or George Guess, a mixed-heritage Cherokee) invented the Cherokee syllabary—a system in which each character represents a syllable. Use of the alphabet resulted in rapid literacy, the spread of Christianity, and printing of the only Native American newspaper—*The Cherokee Phoenix*—in 1828. By 1830, a road system was in place. Many modern highways in North Georgia follow sections of Cherokee roads.

Unfortunately for Native Americans, gold was discovered in North Georgia's Cherokee territory. Georgia passed a law rescinding Cherokee sovereignty and laws, and confiscated their lands, leaving the Principal People at the mercy of greedy settlers and prospectors. The case was appealed to the U.S. Supreme Court and the Cherokees won, but the state of Georgia ignored the court and continued to annex Cherokee lands. President Andrew Jackson did nothing to enforce the Supreme Court's ruling.

Despite the Treaty of New Echota, signed by several prominent chiefs, promising the Indians $5 million in exchange for all their lands east of the Mississippi, Congress used the treaty as a justification for removing the Cherokees in 1838 without any payment. Both U.S. and Georgia troops rounded up 15,000 Cherokees into concentration camps, then herded them along the 2,000-mile Trail of Tears to reservations in Oklahoma. More than half of the displaced Cherokees died on the march from cold, hunger, disease, and enemy Indians. Because the treaty was considered fraudulent by many Cherokees, the chiefs involved in signing it were executed or assassinated, or they died under mysterious circumstances once they reached Oklahoma.

In one of those unfortunate ironies of history, the gold that had caused all this tragedy lasted only a few years, and the area was abandoned by prospectors for richer veins in California.

Today, more than 450 years after de Soto embarked on his search for gold, examples of the great mineral treasures that underlie the area are displayed at the William Weinman Mineral Museum, at I-75 and US 411 near Cartersville, where we will begin following the Chieftains Trail. The museum houses an assortment of local fossils and artifacts dating from the Archaic Period. The museum's Georgia Room showcases minerals from across the state as well as products routinely employed in the tools and handicrafts of the region's original inhabitants.

From the Weinman Mineral Museum, go south on I-75 or US 41 to Cartersville. Visit the Bartow History Center, 319 East Cherokee Avenue, which has displays depicting Native American culture in North Georgia before the white man's arrival.

Remnants of the Mississippian culture are evident in the Etowah Indian Mounds, considered the most-intact Mississippian culture site in the East. To get there, continue through Cartersville onto State 113/State 61, go five miles, then turn left onto Etowah Mounds Road. The Etowah Indians left no written language, but artifacts excavated from the mounds speak a language of their own. These three well-preserved mounds, the ceremonial center of a town of several thousand people, were occupied between A.D. 900 and 1500. The flat-topped earthen knolls, the largest of which is sixty-three feet tall and covers three acres, also served as burial grounds for Indian nobility.

Excavations have revealed that the village was surrounded by a stockade and a deep ditch. Within the walls, the general population built simple huts of wood posts, clay, and thatch.

Several archaeological excavations were made between 1880 and 1953. Since then the state has concentrated on preserving the mounds and developing an interpretive museum. Stairways allow you to climb the mounds without harming the steeply sloping sides. From the top you can see the Etowah Valley for miles in every direction as well as the Etowah River and Pumpkinvine Creek.

In addition to climbing the mounds, you can examine a restored fish trap at the river, take a walk along the riverbank trail, or have a picnic by the river's languid waters.

The interpretive center contains artifacts made from stone, wood, seashells, and copper found in the excavations, as well as life-sized figures, paintings, historical explanations, and an audiovisual show.

From the Etowah Indian Mounds, return to US 411 and proceed west to Rome. The Cchieftains Museum, 501 Riverside Parkway, tells the story of Major Ridge, a prominent Cherokee leader who toiled to conform to the white man's culture while preserving his Indian heritage. He served as a mediator in many disputes with other tribes and earned the rank of major in the Battle of Horseshoe Bend in 1814. He was also one of the signers of the Treaty of New Echota, ceding the Cherokee lands to the state of Georgia.

Ridge's home, Chieftains, is on the banks of the Oostanaula River where Ridge and his family were ferryboat masters, storekeepers, and slaveholding planters. The gracious, white clapboard, nineteenth-century plantation house began life as a simple log cabin in 1794. In 1828, it was expanded into a Piedmont planter's house. After Ridge's removal during the Trail of Tears, the house changed hands numerous times. Union soldiers tried to burn the house in 1864, but it wouldn't ignite. Extensive remodeling in the late 1800s, followed by the addition of two wings in the 1920s, produced the house that you see today.

The museum contains bountiful exhibits describing Cherokee history, Ridge's life, and the history of Northwest Georgia. A restored riverboat, the *Myra H.*, similar to one used by Ridge, is located on the property. An archaeological dig behind the home revealed the original location of the trading post.

Rome has an excellent audiotape describing the city's attractions and its significance in North Georgia's history to accompany the self-guided walking/driving tour. The tape can be borrowed from the Welcome Center, 402 Civic Center Hill.

If you're interested in accommodations, Rome boasts two historic bed and breakfasts—The Chandler Arms, 2 Coral Avenue, and Claremont House, 906 East Second Avenue. In addition, Red Top Mountain Lodge, at Red Top Mountain State Park on Lake Allatoona, offers cottages with kitchen facilities.

Take State 53 north, then turn east on State 140 toward Adairsville. Turn right on Hall Station Road, go 5.5 miles to Barnsley Gardens Road, and turn right. Follow it two miles to the Barnsley Gardens entrance.

After the removal of the Cherokee, one of those to take advantage of the Georgia Land Lottery was Godfrey Barnsley, who acquired 10,000 acres in northern Bartow County south of Adairsville. From the Cherokee wilderness, he created a beautiful estate with an Italianate mansion as the centerpiece of thirty acres of English-style gardens. After the family and estate played a part in the Civil War, there followed years of hardship capped when the villa was destroyed in a 1906 tornado. Recently the gardens of Barnsley Gardens have been restored and opened to the public. For Barnsley Gardens' interesting Civil War history, see the Blue and Gray Trail.

While near Adairsville, you might want to catch a bite at the 1902 Stock Exchange, on the Public Square, or The Adairsville Inn, 100 South Main Street.

Go back to State 140, go east to US 41, then turn north on US 41. Follow it to Calhoun, then turn north on State 225 to New Echota. The legislature of the Cherokee Nation, which covered North Georgia and parts of four other states, established New Echota as its capital in 1825. A thriving town, the governmental seat became headquarters for a small, independent nation. The hamlet, similar to any white village of the period, had a town center surrounded by fifty dwellings and twenty other structures, including stores, government buildings, a gristmill, a sawmill, and outbuildings. Residents grew cotton, and sheep roamed freely.

Once the Cherokee were forced off their lands, the town was gradually destroyed, and even the trees were cut down so more land could be farmed by white settlers. The only structure to survive was the home of missionary Samuel A. Worcester; it has been restored and furnished to represent the period. However, several authentic buildings have been moved from other sites around Georgia, and some buildings have been reconstructed. Although the town is only a ghost of its former glory, visitors can see what it was like.

Beginning at the Visitors Center, tourists can explore the museum and watch an audiovisual presentation. A self-guided walking tour includes an authentic middle-class Cherokee homestead, a reconstruction of the two-story log Council House, the Supreme Courthouse, the Worcester House, Vann's Tavern—the only structure in present-day New Echota that was Cherokee built—the Print Shop, and the Boudinot House site.

If you want to spend the night in the area, Stoneleigh, in Calhoun, is an elegant bed and breakfast at 316 Fain Street.

Return to US 41 and go north to Dalton. Crown Gardens and Archives, 715 Chattanooga Avenue, displays a collection of Indian artifacts.

From Dalton, take I-75 north to State 2, then proceed west to US 27 and turn north. Located near Rossville, at the Georgia/Tennessee border, is the John Ross House, on McFarland Avenue, a memorial to the greatest Cherokee chief. The two-story log house was built in 1797 by John McDonald, Ross's maternal grandfather, using plank flooring, rock chimneys, and pegged construction.

While in this area, two exquisite places to stay are the Gordon-Lee Mansion in Chickamauga or Captain's Quarters in Fort Oglethorpe—both bed and breakfasts.

Return south via I-75 and turn east on US 76 toward Chatsworth. Turn south on State 225. At the intersection of State 225 and State 52 is the Chief Vann House. Known as the showplace of the Cherokee Nation, it is a two-story Federal-style brick mansion built by Chief James Vann in 1804. Once called Diamond Hill, it was the center of a large, prosperous plantation with mills, ferries, taverns, and slaves. The house features an elaborately cantilevered stairway, the oldest example of cantilevered construction in Georgia, and is furnished with many fine antiques. Georgia's state flower—the Cherokee rose—"blooms" continuously at the chief's house, because he had craftsmen carve the dainty flower into the moldings. Also on the property is the log cabin in which Vann originally lived.

Vann contributed to the education of the Cherokee leaders by inviting Moravian missionaries to teach them. He supported Christianity as a means of progress for his people. During Vann House Days, the third weekend in July, demonstrations of living history are presented on the grounds.

The elegant Chief Vann House built by a Cherokee chief in 1805

Candlelight tours are conducted the second weekend in December.

Go east on State 52 to Fort Mountain State Park. Fort Mountain derives its name from an ancient 855-foot-long rock wall that stands at the highest point of the mountain. The mysterious wall is thought to have been built by Indians as a ceremonial center more than a thousand years ago. The park offers picnicking, camping, cottages, swimming, hiking, and spectacular views. Guided nature walks to the mysterious wall are conducted in August, and an overnight backcountry trip is made in October.

An alternative for accommodations is Cohutta Lodge, a mountaintop retreat.

Continue east on State 52, then turn south at Ellijay onto State 515. Turn east onto State 53 to Tate. An area along the banks of Long Swamp Creek near Tate was a prominent Cherokee village until their forced resettlement in the 1830s. Only remnants of the Old Harnago Tavern and The Tate Spring House—one of the oldest buildings in North Georgia—survive.

The property now contains the Tate House—better known as the Pink Marble Mansion—a 17,000-square-foot manor built in 1926 by Col. Sam Tate, president of the Georgia Marble Company, to showcase the marble from his nearby quarries. Today the Tate House is an opulent bed and breakfast, restaurant, and tavern. A complete resort, the Tate House property also features cabins, a swimming pool, tennis, and horseback riding. This is a good place to complete your tour, get a meal, and/or spend the night.

Or you can continue south on State 53 and turn east at State 372 to Ball Ground. A historical marker identifies the Talivsa Cherokee battleground. Today Ball Ground is a quaint, century-old town nestled in the foothills of the Blue Ridge Mountains. From here, it's easy to get on I-575 south to Atlanta.

There is one other site on the Chieftains Trail—The McIntosh Reserve. Although it is so far removed from those previously described that it might be more practical to explore on a different trip, here's its history.

Chief William McIntosh was the son of a full-blooded Creek mother and a Scottish father. Raised as an Indian, McIntosh became a chief aligned with the Lower Creek faction and operated a backwoods plantation, tavern, and ferry on the Chattahoochee River at Whitesburg, south of Carrollton and I-20. McIntosh was one of those murdered for his part in the Treaty of New Echota and the resulting Trail of Tears. Although none of McIntosh's buildings survive, visitors can camp, hike, and picnic at the McIntosh Reserve. If you're in the area but prefer not to camp, an excellent choice of accommodations is Twin Oaks B&B, a private cottage on a country estate at 9565 East Liberty Road.

There are Indian sites on each of the trails described in this book, with the most prominent sites described in the chapters on the Antebellum Trail, the Chattahoochee Trace, and the Peach Blossom Trail.

While you are exploring North Georgia's Indian heritage, take the time and a few detours to see what else the region has to offer. See the Blue and Gray Trail for information on Civil War sites in this area.

Scenic drives in the North Georgia mountains include the Lookout Mountain Parkway, Ridge and Valley Byway, and several self-driving tours developed by Fannin County.

The Northwest Georgia mountain region contains a large portion of the Chattahoochee National Forest, several state parks, lakes, parts of the Appalachian Trail, and numerous waterfalls.

Unique experiences such as llama trekking, eagle watching, gold panning, spelunking, and white-water rafting await adventurers in Northwest Georgia.

Special events occur throughout the year: the Prater's Mill Country Fair in May and October; reenactments of the Civil War Battles of Resaca, Rome, and Tunnel Hill; Finster Festival;

The Appalachian Trail begins atop Springer Mountain

Mayfest on the Rivers; Ellijay Apple Festival; Heritage Holidays; and Coosa River Christmas.

All types of lodging can be found: hotels, motels, mountain lodges, cabins, cottages, campgrounds, and intimate bed and breakfasts. Shops and restaurants offer something for everyone. Flammini's Cafe Italia, in Dalton, specializes in gourmet Italian dishes.

Although antiques can be found everywhere throughout the region, Summerville and Cave Spring have an abundance of antique shops. In Dalton, "Carpet Capital of the World," you can find dozens of carpet showrooms and outlets. Dalton also sports two outlet malls. Mountain arts and crafts are widely available.

Northwest Georgia's plethora of Native American sites and other attractions will keep you coming back again and again—for a day, a week, a month, maybe forever.

In the Area

Barnsley Gardens, 597 Barnsley Gardens Road, Adairsville, GA 30103, 404-773-7480.

Bartow History Center, 319 East Cherokee Avenue, Cartersville, GA 30120, 404-382-3818.

Blue Ridge Visitor Center, Appalachian Highway (US 76), Blue Ridge, GA 30513, 706-632f-5680.

Calhoun Local Welcome Center, 300 South Wall Street, Calhoun, GA, 30701, 706-625-3200.

Carroll County Convention and Visitors Bureau, 200 Northside Drive, Carrollton, GA 30117, 800-292-0871.

Cartersville-Bartow County Tourism Council, P.O. Box 200397, Cartersville, GA 30120, 800-733-2280 or 404-387-1357

Chatsworth Local Welcome Center, US 52, Chatsworth, GA 30705, 706-695-6060.

Chattooga County Chamber of Commerce, 106 West Washington Street, Summerville, GA 30747, 404-857-4033.

Chatsworth-Murray County Chamber of Commerce, P.O. Box 327, Chatsworth, GA 30705, 706-695-6060.

Chieftains Trail Council, P.O. Box 5823, Rome, GA 30161, 706-295-5576.

Dade Development Corp., Box 849, Trenton, GA 30752, 706-657-7513.

Dalton-Whitfield Convention and Visitors Bureau, 2211 Dug Gap Battle Road, Dalton, GA 30720, 706-272-7676.

Etowah Mounds State Historic Site, 813 Indian Mounds Road, S.W., Cartersville, GA 30120, 404-387-3747.

Gordon County Chamber of Commerce, 300 South Wall Street, Calhoun, GA 30701, 706-625-3200.

LaFayette Chamber of Commerce, Box 985, LaFayette, GA 30728, 706-638-1930.

Marietta Welcome Center and Visitors Bureau, No. 4 Depot Street/Suite B, Marietta, GA 30060, 404-429-1115.

New Echota Historic Site, 1211 Chatsworth Highway, Calhoun, GA 30701, 706-629-8151.

Greater Rome Convention and Visitor Bureau, P.O. Box 5823, Rome, GA 30162, 706-295-5576 or 800-444-1834.

Rome Local Welcome Center, Civic Center Hill, Rome, GA 30161, 800-444-1834.

William Weinman Mineral Museum, Mineral Museum Drive, Cartersville, GA 30120, 404-386-0576.

6 ~

Classic

Magnolias

Getting there: Take US 129 to Hawkinsville.

Highlights: *Racehorses and the Hawkinsville Harness Festival, bird dogs and the Georgia Field Trials, Stuckey's Candy, Vidalia onions, camellias, the Masters Gold Tournament, and Augusta's Riverwalk.*

Standardbred horses, cutting horses, champion bird dogs, and fox hunts vie for your attention with antebellum architecture and Civil War history. Golf and fishing are major temptations. Pecans, kiwifruit, and Vidalia onions tantalize your taste buds. Permeating everything is the sweet scent of camellias and magnolias. This attraction-packed route takes you 250 miles across both the Magnolia Midlands and Classic South regions of Georgia—hence the name Classic Magnolias.

Elegant Standardbred horses, manes flying, strut gracefully around the red clay track pulling picturesque sulkies and drivers dressed in colorful silks. You might imagine you've been plunked down at the Red Mile Race Track in Lexington or at the Belmont in Saratoga, New York. In reality you're in Hawkinsville—since 1894 the winter home and training ground of many of North America's finest pacers and trotters.

The moderate climate and excellent track surface of high-quality Georgia red clay make Hawkinsville an ideal spot for northerners to ensure year-round race training for their horses.

The Hawkinsville Harness Training Facility is on US 129 south of town. More than 350 horse owners and trainers and their magnificent steeds populate Hawkinsville from October to May. You can drop by anytime, although the horses are most likely to be training outdoors early in the morning.

The forerunner of the Hawkinsville Harness Festival started back in 1894 when the Wiregrass Exposition was organized. Men could decide once and for all who had the best horse, women showed off their needlework, merchants displayed their wares, and folks came from miles around to watch the races. The present-day week-long event, held in early April, has been chosen as one of the Top Twenty Festivals in the Southeast by the Southeast Tourism Society. Festivities include a beauty pageant, golf tournament, flea market, arts and crafts, tours of some of Hawkinsville's stately homes, the Spring Pig Ribbin' Cookoff, and two days of racing.

The Hawkinsville/Pulaski County Chamber of Commerce, on Lumpkin Street, provides an excellent map to guide you on a driving tour of more than fifty historic buildings, some dating back to 1824. One of these sumptuous homes has been converted into an elegant bed and breakfast. Called The Black Swan Inn, the establishment also has a fine restaurant. Named for one of the last steamboats on the Ocmulgee River, the inn is located at 411 Progress Avenue, which is also US 341/State 247. Another architecturally significant building is the 1907 Historic Opera House, at the corner of Broad and Lumpkin Streets, where cultural performances are held throughout the year.

Food will tempt you to visit two other attractions. Gooseneck Farms, five miles south of town on Abbeville Highway, packages pecans and pecan candies as well as other southern specialties. You can purchase these delicacies from their shop, Nut House in the Grove, on US 129, two miles south of town. Double Q Farms, on State 26, grows kiwifruit—in fact, it is the state's largest producer of kiwis—and creates fine jams.

Take US 341 east to Eastman, original home of Stuckey's Candy—a variety of confections created around pecans. You can visit the pecan orchards and the candy shop. Get a brochure for the Eastman/Dodge Driving Tour from the Welcome Center, 407 College Street. Dodge Hill B&B, 105 Ninth Street, offers homey accommodations.

From Eastman, take US 341/US 23 to McRae. The town's best-known achievement was the catch of the world record largemouth bass—a 22-pound, 4-ounce giant caught in Montgomery Lake off the Ocmulgee River in 1932. Countless fishermen since have tried in vain to beat the record.

Talmadge Home, on US 341, was the home of two former Georgia governors—father and son—Eugene Talmadge and Herman Eugene Talmadge. Nearby, the Old South Georgia College Auditorium, built in 1893, serves as the cultural center of the community. Perhaps McRae's most unusual feature is the half-size replica of the Statue of Liberty, located in Liberty Square. Also in the square are a Liberty Bell, which served as the town fire bell at the turn of the century, and a Veterans Memorial.

Leave McRae on US 280 and head east for Vidalia—world-renowned for its sweet Vidalia onions that grow only within a small area of Georgia. Tours of local onion farms and processing and packaging plants can be arranged in the spring. You can visit tobacco and cotton farms in the fall.

Prominent buildings in town include the Peterson-Wilbanks House, 404 Jackson Street, a 1916 Neoclassical mansion that is now used for law offices; the Ladson Genealogical Library, at 119 Church Street, which contains an impressive archive; and the Altama Art and History Gallery, at Jackson and Sixth Streets. The 1911 structure houses a permanent collection of porcelain and hosts traveling art shows.

Continue on US 280 east to US 1 at Lyons, then go north about 60 miles to Louisville, which served as the first permanent capital of Georgia from 1796 to 1807. The 1758 Old Market House, located in the center of Broad Street, was constructed at the site where two major Native American trading routes crossed. The current courthouse, built in 1904, is on the site of the original state house. Thirty graves of notable Revolutionary War soldiers and a U.S. congressman are located in the Old Cemetery on State 24 east.

Take State 24 east to Waynesboro, where you can visit the Burke County Museum, at 536 Liberty Street. Located in a restored 1859 home, the museum features early history of the county as well as the history of cotton. Waynesboro is known as the Bird Dog Capital of the World because the annual Georgia Field Trials, one of the nation's oldest hunting dog competitions, is held there. If you want to be pampered, stay at Georgia's Guest Bed and Breakfast, 640 East Seventh Street.

Turn north on US 25 to Augusta. Anyone who can spell golf knows about Augusta's Masters Golf Tournament, held annually at the Augusta National Country Club. What few potential travelers realize is that Augusta has many other attractions and exciting events. Located at the Piedmont

For decades, golfers have teed off in Augusta

fall line, Augusta was considered "upcountry" by coastal colonists.

Start at the historic Cotton Exchange. This beautifully restored building serves as a welcome center and museum at the Eighth Street entrance to the Riverwalk complex.

When cotton was king, the Cotton Exchange was one of the busiest buildings in town. Buyers, sellers, and brokers gathered to make deals and fortunes. The room is filled with cotton planting, picking, weighing, and shipping memorabilia; old adding machines; and the rocking chairs and checker tables that served as recreation when trading was slow.

Before leaving the Cotton Exchange, check with the friendly staff for suggestions on things to do and places to stay, shop, or eat.

Outside the Cotton Exchange is the courtyard—paved with bricks embossed with "Augusta"—that leads to the Riverwalk. Lining this courtyard are old cotton warehouses that have been rejuvenated and transformed into boutiques and restaurants.

A fountain erupting from the courtyard paving is an irresistible lure for children of all ages to run through, especially during a hot spell. The Riverwalk is a gigantic park created from a flood-prevention levee along the Augusta Canal. The top of the levee is paved, and both its land- and riverside slopes are luxuriantly landscaped. Various overlooks and benches invite strollers to contemplate the languidly flowing water. Concerts and other entertainment are frequently offered in the waterside amphitheater.

The Morris Museum of Art, at Tenth Street and Riverwalk, houses several permanent collections: southern art, Civil War art, southern impressionism, and the Black presence in southern painting.

Experience the river itself aboard the *Princess Augusta*, a paddle wheeler that tours the river. A rowing regatta and two powerboat races draw international crowds to the Savannah River.

If you can tear yourself away from the river, Augusta has several historic sights you shouldn't miss. Sacred Heart Cultural Arts Center, Greene and Thirteenth Streets, was once a grand Romanesque Revival Catholic Church. The majestic structure now serves as the hub for the arts in Augusta—housing offices of the ballet, symphony, theater, and other cultural groups. Visitors are welcome to browse through the building, inspecting the ornate brickwork on the exterior and the opulent stained-glass windows, marble, and carvings on the interior.

Hidden away near Thirteenth Street and Walton Way is Meadow Garden, the former home of George Walton—one of Georgia's three signers of the Declaration of Independence. Other house museums include the Ezekiel Harris Home, at 1840 Broad Street; Woodrow Wilson Boyhood Home, at 419 Seventh Street; Lucy Laney House, at 116 Phillips Street; and Appleby House, 2260 Walton Way. Other historic buildings open to the public are the Old Medical College, the Government House, and the Augusta-Richmond County Museum—all on Telfair Street.

Just off the Augusta Canal, at 1717 Goodrich Street, is a 176-foot chimney—all that remains of the major Confederate Powderworks, which once made Augusta so important to the Confederacy. The only remaining structure commissioned by the Confederacy, the powderworks produced 2.3 million pounds of gunpowder during its three-year operation. Cartridges, grenades, and other arms for the Confederacy were manufactured at Augusta College, 2500 Walton Way. Augusta's Civil War monument, in the center of Broad Street between Seventh and Eighth Streets, recognizes the importance of the common soldier by depicting a private at the top and the generals around the bottom. Two other monuments are the Haunted Pillar, at Fifth and Broad, the only landmark left after an itinerant preacher put a curse on the market-place, and the Signer's Monument, at Greene and Gwinnett Streets, dedicated to Georgia's signers of the Declaration of Independence.

Bishop Leonidas Polk, "fighting bishop of the Confederacy," is buried beneath the altar of St. Paul's Episcopal Church, 605 Reynolds Street. Used as Confederate hospitals were Holy Trinity Catholic Church, 720 Telfair Street; the First Presbyterian Church, 642 Telfair Street; and the Young Men's Library, on Telfair Street.

During the late 1800s and through the turn of the century, Augusta prospered and attracted residents and tourists to the cool heights of Walton Way. A drive through the Summerville/Gould's Corner neighborhoods is like entering a time warp, where Greek Revival mansions compete for your attention with Italian Renaissance Victorians.

The charming Partridge Inn, 2110 Walton Way, which began as a private residence in 1879, was continually enlarged until it became one of the country's first all-suite inns. Faithfully restored and graciously furnished, the inn boasts a quarter mile of porches and private balconies. It is one of only two historic hotels in Georgia invited to belong to the prestigious Historic Hotels of America. You can hardly imagine anything more southern than relaxing in a rocker with a tall cool drink on one of the endless verandas.

A delightful concept led to the creation of the Clarion Telfair Inn, on Telfair Street. The company purchased and restored an entire square block of turn-of-the-century houses to use as hotel rooms. Think what fun you could have staying in a different house each time. The inn also has a small conference center, restaurant, and cocktail lounge.

Down the street, at 836 Green Street, is the Telfair Inn's sister property, The Oglethorpe Inn—a bed and breakfast contained in two adjoining historic homes.

Excluding the Masters Golf Tournament, the city's premier event is the Augusta Futurity—the largest cutting horse tournament east of the Mississippi and one of the top ten in the world.

From Augusta, take US 278/US 78 west to Thomson. Early settlers were Quakers who came in 1768, making it the southern-most Quaker settlement in the country. Thomson is called "The Camellia City of the South" because the climate is perfect for growing the beautiful plant; houses and gardens overflow with the vibrant blooms.

The focal point of historic downtown Thomson is the Depot, which houses the Thomson/McDuffie Tourism Bureau, where you can get a brochure for a self-guided driving tour. In front of the depot is Women of the Sixties—a monument to women who loyally supported the South during and after the Civil War.

The Rock House, built from fieldstone in 1785, is Georgia's oldest documented dwelling. Drive by Hickory Hill, home of Sen. Tom Watson, who established the rural free delivery system. The guided Upcountry Plantation Tour includes, among other plantation homes, The Rock House and Alexandria—an elegant 1805 Virginia-style house surrounded by boxwood gardens.

Thomson is the center of fox hunting country. From November through March, the Belle Meade Hunt rides to the hounds. Visitors are welcome.

Two bed and breakfasts are located in historic houses: Four Chimneys B&B, 2316 Wire Road, and 1810 West Inn, 254 North Seymour Drive.

Leave Thomson by turning north onto US 78 and continue to Washington—"where Dixie died." The sobriquet was earned when Confederate president Jefferson Davis held his last cabinet meeting here while fleeing from pursuing Union troops. He was captured a few days later at Irwinville. Washington was created one year after the Declaration of Independence was signed and was the first town in the country named in honor of George Washington.

Native son Robert Toombs was briefly the Confederacy's secretary of state before he resigned to take a commission in the Army of Northern Virginia. Toombs must have had a very cantankerous nature. A successful planter and lawyer before the war, he had a turbulent career as a legislator. During the Civil War, he resigned from his military commission, retreated to his home, and spent the rest of the war criticizing the Confederate government. Then he escaped from Union troops sent to arrest him and fled into foreign exile. When he returned two years later, he still refused to take an oath of allegiance to the United States—earning him the name "the South's unreconstructed rebel." The 1797 Robert Toombs Home, at 216 East Robert Toombs Avenue, is a state historic site. A film depicts Toombs as an old man telling his story to a young reporter.

The Washington Historical Museum, at 308 East Robert Toombs Avenue, is located in a magnificently restored and furnished Greek Revival home built in 1835. Among the special exhibits are historic memorabilia including Jefferson Davis's camp desk, a gift from English sympathizers and used by him until the last cabinet meeting. Diaries, newspapers, and letters, as well as a Confederate gun collection and a variety of Indian artifacts, are displayed.

The Zirbess-Ledbetter House, at 104 East Liberty Street, is another fine example of Greek Revival architecture. Built in 1905, it now houses city offices and the Chamber of Commerce.

One of the most striking architectural gems in town is the Mary Willis Library, at Liberty and Jefferson Streets. Built in

1888 in High Victorian style with Tiffany windows, it was the first free library in Georgia.

You can look back at early American life at Callaway Plantation, on US 78. The working plantation has five historic houses, including the Greek Revival Brick House (1869), the Log Cabin (1785), a two-story Federal Plain-style house, a country store, and a blacksmith shop—all furnished to illustrate life in various periods of history.

If you want to spend the night in or near Washington, call Blackmon B&B, a restored 1786 farmhouse at 512 North Alexander Avenue, or Holly Ridge Country Inn, at 2221 Sandtown Road, a charming hostelry created by connecting a primitive 1780s farmhouse with a grand 1880s Victorian house.

In the Area

Augusta-Richmond County Convention and Visitors Bureau, 32 Eighth Street, Suite 200, Augusta, GA 30901, 706-823-6600 or 800-726-0243.

Eastman/Dodge County Chamber of Commerce and Local Welcome Center, 407 College Street, Eastman, GA 31023, 912-374-4723.

Hawkinsville-Pulaski County Chamber of Commerce, 100 Lumpkin Street, Hawkinsville, GA 31036, 912-783-1717.

Thomson-McDuffie County Tourism, Convention and Visitors Bureau, 111 Railroad Street Depot, Thomson, GA 30824, 706-595-5584.

Washington-Wilkes County Chamber of Commerce, 104 East Liberty Street, Washington, GA 30673, 706-678-2013.

7 ~

Coasting Along Georgia's Seaboard

Getting there: Take US 17 south out of Savannah.

Highlights: *Historic plantations; the Okefenokee Swamp; Savannah's roundhouse, Black History Museum, and historic district; coastal towns; and sugar mill ruins.*

The existence of barrier islands presupposes a coastline for them to protect. However, the attractions of Georgia's Golden Isles are so alluring, the state's mainland coast is often ignored or neglected. If asked to identify a coastal town, most residents and visitors could name Savannah but would then be stumped. They might be able to recognize Brunswick as the "Gateway to the Golden Isles," but be ignorant of its charms.

We weren't much different until we wandered the southern part of the state. Pleasant surprises await those willing to search for them.

Georgia has a 100-mile sweep of coastline on the Atlantic Ocean. If bays, offshore islands, and river mouths are included, the coastline measures 2,344 miles.

In the peaceful haven that is the coast, you'll find lengthy, meandering rivers cutting the level, prolific forestland, forming highways that pierced the interior for early settlers and providing pleasure paths for today's travelers.

Hypnotizing marshes, undulating oceans of cordgrass, moss-draped live oaks, and spiky palmettos guard historic sites. Here soldiers, slaves, Indians, pirates, and timber barons once flourished. Remains of rice plantations and forts coexist with metropolitan delights such as down-home and sophisticated dining, multiple cultural events, bargain and upscale shopping, and a wide range of accommodations. You'll find state parks, campgrounds, chain motels, and elegant bed and breakfasts.

Although I-95 runs north-south from Savannah to the Florida border, why not take the scenic route along US 17 as it winds past Richmond Hill, Midway, Sunbury, Darien, Brunswick, and St. Marys?

Farther inland you can explore the mysteries of the Okefenokee Swamp, as well as the small towns of Folkston, Fargo, and Waycross.

Begin your tour in Savannah. This gracious city, where the nostalgic charm and elegance of the Old South are portrayed with carriage rides and tours of historic homes and inns, deserves a chapter or a book of its own, but we'll hit some highlights.

Savannah was carved from the wilderness in 1733, when English Gen. James Oglethorpe founded the first city in the Georgia colony. It served as the temporary state capital from 1733 to 1782. The strategic location on Yamacraw Bluff overlooking the Savannah River created a buffer between rich Carolina tobacco fields and Spanish invaders in Florida.

Early colonists tried to grow silk, but its production never became a major factor in the economy. When cotton became king, Savannah boomed as a port city.

Oglethorpe's careful plan for the city remains one of Savannah's most enduring and alluring features. The city was laid out on a grid with twenty-four parklike squares. These same squares today abound with mature, moss-draped live oaks that create a green canopy over shiny magnolias, brilliant azaleas, and prominent monuments and fountains.

Around the squares, stately homes, churches, and businesses blossomed. During the 1950s some of these treasures were lost in the name of progress. However, in 1966, a 2.2-square-mile area was designated as a National Historic Landmark District—one of the largest in the country. Almost 1,500 structures have been saved and rehabilitated.

Begin a tour of Savannah by visiting the Central of Georgia Railroad Station, an 1860 depot that houses the Savannah Visitors Center, where you get brochures and advice. Next door is the Central of Georgia Railroad Roundhouse Complex, the oldest and most complete locomotive repair shop and roundhouse in the country.

The tourist heart of Savannah lies along the river on River Street and Factors Walk. A nine-block area of warehouses was restored and now contains shops, galleries, restaurants, and nightspots. Riverwalk Plaza is a delightful meeting or people-watching spot. This is the place to catch a sight-seeing cruise aboard the paddle wheelers *Savannah River Queen* and *First Lady of Savannah*. Two inns right on the river are the Olde Harbor Inn, 508 East Factors Walk, and the River Street Inn, 115 East River Street. Just across East Bay Street are the East Bay Inn and the Mulberry Inn.

Savannah has a significant Black history. That heritage can be explored at the King-Tisdell Cottage of Black History Museum, 514 East Huntingdon Street, an outstanding historic project of the Georgia Trust for Historic Preservation, and the

Beach Institute, 502 East Harris Street. Pick up the brochure "Negro Heritage Trail," which presents three separate walking or driving tours.

Saint Patrick's Day and Christmas celebrations in Savannah, the "Hostess City of the South," rival those of New Orleans, well known as a party city. The second-largest Saint Patrick's Day celebration in the country takes place in Savannah, which hosts 300,000 people every year for the wearin' of the green. Savannah's festival and parade are popular, so you need to make hotel reservations at least a year in advance. Many lodgings, in fact, require a prepaid, three-night minimum stay. This is one time that guaranteeing your room by credit card probably won't do. Innkeepers want cash, up front. If you have trouble getting reservations, try surrounding towns for accommodations.

Savannah was the home of James Lord Pierpont when he wrote "Jingle Bells" in 1859. The Jingle Bells Festival is a month-long jubilee in his honor.

The profusion of blooms in late spring is the signal for the Tour of Homes and Gardens. Several other popular festivals keep things hopping all year in Savannah.

The city boasts a potpourri of delightful inns and bed and breakfasts—too many to mention here. Several reservation services can help you choose the best inn for you: R.S.V.P. Georgia and Savannah, 800-729-7787, and Savannah Historic Inns and Guest Houses, 912-233-7666.

You'll never run out of outstanding places to eat in Savannah. Elizabeth's on 37th, at 105 East Thirty-seventh, has been named one of the Top 25 Restaurants in America. Garibaldi, 315 West Congress Street, serves local seafood specials. You can order contemporary and colonial Georgian cuisine at The Olde Pink House, 23 Abercorn Street, one of Savannah's oldest mansions. The restaurant at the 17 Hundred 90 Inn, 307 East President Street, serves Continental cuisine and has earned numerous awards, including The Most Elegant

Restaurant in Savannah from *Gourmet* magazine. Pirates House, which specializes in seafood, is located in an authentic 1733 tavern at 20 East Broad Street. In the lower level of a modest townhouse on Jones Street is Mrs. Wilkes Boarding House, a world-famous, all-you-can-eat, family-style restaurant.

South of Savannah on US 17 is Richmond Hill. Located on the south bank of the Great Ogeechee River is Fort McAllister, built in 1861. The best-preserved earthwork fortification of the Confederacy, it withstood nine naval assaults in two years, including one during the defense of Savannah. It ultimately fell to Union Gen. William Tecumseh Sherman's land-based bayonet charge in December of 1864, opening the way for his conquest of Savannah. A museum commemorates the fort's contributions to the Southern effort. Now a historic state park, it has tent and trailer sites, a boat dock and ramp, nature trails, and fishing. Adjacent Richmond Hill State Park offers similar facilities.

The tiny town of Midway, on US 17, boasts Midway Church, built by the Puritans in 1729. Its congregation spawned two signers of the Declaration of Independence, two Revolutionary War generals, and a U.S. senator. The church was occupied by Sherman's troops in 1864. Next door, a raised cottage has been transformed into a museum housing furniture, artifacts, and documents representing the early eighteenth to the mid-nineteenth centuries.

Take a detour west of US 17 via US 84 to Hinesville. Founded in 1835, the town features a charmingly restored Main Street shopping district, the historic courthouse and Court Street neighborhood, attractively landscaped parks, and many restaurants. Upon its completion in 1882, the Old

Liberty County Jail was described as "a handsome structure with all the modern conveniences"—running water, plumbing, fireplaces, twelve-inch-thick brick walls, and thirty-six-inch-thick concrete floors.

Nearby the Victory Museum at Fort Stewart houses weapons, uniforms, flags, equipment, vehicles, and historic photos from the Civil War to the present. A special collection focuses on Merrill's Marauders.

Retrace US 84 past US 17 and I-95 to Sunbury. Once a bustling colonial seaport, Georgia's second largest after Savannah, Sunbury is now just a drowsy footnote to history. Important Revolutionary War and War of 1812 battles were fought here. The visitors center displays the history of earthen Fort Morris and the town of Sunbury. Fort Defiance, built during the War of 1812, still stands and features a museum, slide show, and scenic view.

Fort Morris Historic Site, seven miles east of I-95, is a revolutionary earthwork fortification. Attractions include a museum, exhibits, and a walking tour.

Return to US 17 and proceed south to Darien. Though small, the town has a mighty history. Georgia's second-oldest town, it was founded by Gen. James Oglethorpe's Scottish Highlanders. It once rivaled Philadelphia in banking and led the world in timber exports. Unfortunately, all but a church and one other building were destroyed during the Civil War.

Fort King George, 1.5 miles north of US 17, was the southernmost outpost of the British colonies in 1721; predating the English, the area had been an Indian village and a Spanish mission. The reconstructed blockhouse is a repository of early British lore as well as that of the Creek and Guale (pronounced wally) Indians. Costumed guides provide living history.

Darien blossomed at the turn of the century. You'll want to wander the historic squares, the district of impressive timber barons' mansions, and The Ridge—an area of sea captains' homes. Modern-day enterprises include shrimping and caviar processing. If you plan your visit for spring, you can watch the engaging ceremony of Blessing the Fleet.

Open Gates, on Vernon Square, offers elegant bed and breakfast accommodations in a restored home that was built in 1876 by a timber baron.

South of Darien on US 17 stands Hofwyl-Broadfield Plantation, which stayed in the same family from 1807 to 1973, when it was willed to the state. It operated as a rice plantation until 1915. Here you can see rice dikes as well as the typical Low Country architecture of the antebellum plantation house and outbuildings. Surrounded by ancient live oaks, magnolias, and camellias, the house is furnished with fine antiques. In the museum you can examine a model of a working rice plantation and other exhibits, as well as watch a slide show about the life of planters and slaves.

Continue south on US 17 to Brunswick. For those who've often breezed through or around the town on the way to the Golden Isles, treat yourself to a stop here. Old Town Brunswick, listed on the National Register of Historic Places, was laid out in a grid pattern in 1771 with broad streets and generous parks. Street names reflect both British and German ties. Thirty-six architecturally significant sites are keyed to a driving tour available at Old City Hall or from the Brunswick-Golden Isles Local Welcome Center. In addition to early colonial architecture, many fine examples of the Victorian style grace the town.

Nature is also on display in Brunswick. From Overlook Park, survey the Marshes of Glynn, immortalized by Georgia's greatest poet, Sidney Lanier. Under the Lanier Oak on

US 17, he was inspired to write some of his finest poetry. According to legend, an Indian lover and his maiden met under the Lover's Oak—now 900 years old—located at modern-day Albany and Prince Streets.

A fishing village and port since its founding, Brunswick retains that tradition. The picturesque shrimp fleet of the "world's shrimp capital" can be seen from Bay Street between Gloucester and Prince Streets. The Blessing of the Fleet occurs on Mother's Day weekend.

In Brunswick, an excellent choice for accommodations is 1886 Brunswick Manor B&B, at 825 Egmont Street, and its next-door sister, the 1890 House. Rose Manor Guest House, circa 1890, is a Victorian cottage at 1108 Richmond Street.

Just before you reach the Florida border on US 17, turn east on State 40 to St. Marys, tucked away between the marsh, the St. Marys River, and the Intracoastal Waterway. When Florida still belonged to Spain, St. Marys was the southernmost port in the United States. A legacy of that time was the use of ballast stones in the building foundations. Ships threw the stones overboard when they picked up cargo in St. Marys.

Despite the buildup of nearby Kings Bay naval submarine base, the Atlantic Coast headquarters of the Trident nuclear submarine fleet, St. Marys retains its classic small southern village flavor. An infusion of workers has increased the size of the town, but the core historic district survives virtually untouched.

Timucua, Creek, Yamacraw, and Guale Indians were the first residents. Jean Ribault, a French Huguenot, sailed up the brooding St. Marys River in 1562, but it wasn't until 1787 that the town, perched on Buttermilk Bluff above the river, was founded. The streets in this twenty-block historic area retain

*Twisted, gnarled live oaks draped with Spanish moss flourish
between Savannah and the St. Marys River*

the names of the twenty men who purchased plots of land to form the town.

The focal point of St. Marys is the waterfront. A pavilion provides shade for fishermen or tourists who come to watch the shrimp boats, pleasure craft, and charter boats or to wait for *The Cumberland Queen,* the daily ferry to Cumberland Island (see Golden Isles).

The day of George Washington's burial at Mt. Vernon, St. Marys citizens held a symbolic funeral, buried a casket, and planted six oak trees on the median of Osborne Street. Only one oak survived; it became the symbol of the city. When the tree died, after about a century, the wood was given to the U.S. Navy for use in repairs of the *USS Constitution,* "Old Ironsides." The stump remains.

Among the live oaks and aged cedars are buildings that have prevailed against wars, tidal waves, hurricanes, floods, and fires. The oldest structure is the 1801 Jackson-Clark-Bessent-MacDonnel House, on Osborne Street. Across the street is Orange Hall. Named for the orange trees around it, the magnificent antebellum mansion is reputed to be one of the finest examples of Greek Revival architecture in the South. Built between 1829 and 1834, it now houses the welcome center.

During the Civil War, the chapel of the Methodist Church was occupied by federal troops and used as a quartermaster's depot where animals were butchered.

There's an amusing story about the Presbyterian Church. Early smugglers were unable to get their stolen goods ashore because of vigilant citizens, so the smugglers stole the minister's horse and hoisted it into the church belfry. While the entire populace was trying to figure out how to get the horse down, the smugglers brought their contraband ashore and disappeared.

The Oak Grove Cemetery, incorporated in the initial city plan, holds graves of soldiers from every war that this nation has fought as well as settlers from early Camden County, including Acadians who settled here in 1799 after escaping their native Nova Scotia.

As federal troops departed during the Civil War, they burned virtually the entire town. One report stated that soldiers "gutted every house abandoned by its owner, carried off everything moveable and destroyed the rest." Reconstruction was a hard time for residents, but gradually the town came back to life and a new industry emerged—cutting crossties from the vast supply of pines. Many were used in the construction of the Panama Canal.

Unique to St. Marys is a Braille Trail. Historic markers use Braille as well as traditional signage to identify thirty-eight historically significant buildings and sites with their names and date of construction. St. Marys Braille Trail has more Braille signs than any other city in the country and is the only community in the Southeast with these signs.

The famous Toonerville Trolley is a lighthearted stop on Osborne Street. Built in 1928 to carry passengers to and from the north-south rail line in Kingsland, it had the body of a truck but ran on tracks. The trolley and several local landmarks gained national fame when cartoonist Roy Crane began his cartoon strip "Wash Tubbs and Easy" in 1935.

The McIntosh Sugar Mill Tabby Ruin is the largest and most well preserved tabby structure on the coast. Reached by Spur 40, it is just across from Kings Bay's main gate. Tabby, distinctive to the southern coast, is a strong construction material made from a mixture of ground oyster shells, sand, water, and lime formed from burned oyster shells. The building, site of John McIntosh's Sugar Mill, contains rooms depicting cane grinding, boiling, and processing of sugar products.

Historic St. Marys boasts two charming bed and breakfasts right on Osborne Street—both within easy walking distance of the pier: the restored 1870 Goodbread House and the 1872 Historic Spencer House Inn. Another choice of accommodations is the Riverview Hotel, built in 1916 across the street from the pier. Seagle's, the hotel's restaurant, serves seafood and charbroiled steak and will pack ample picnic lunches for guests, perhaps to spend the day at Cumberland Island or the Okefenokee Swamp.

Near St. Marys on Spur 40, Crooked River State Park provides cabins, camping facilities, a boat ramp, swimming, a playground, ball field, and hiking trails.

After completing the coast, you may want to explore the region inland. The most novel experience you can have is to visit the primeval Okefenokee Swamp—"America's greatest natural botanical garden." Dense, dim, and mysterious, but rarely dangerous, the swamp is one of nature's most peculiar creations.

Two rivers, the Suwannee and the St. Marys, constantly flush and rejuvenate the shallow, 950-square-mile depression, the largest swamp in the United States. A profusion of vegetation, fish, bird, and animal life—many species bordering on extinction—thrives within the area.

Among towering, thick stands of cypress are scattered smooth, unobstructed plains, called prairies, flecked with herbage that only looks firm. One step and you'll see why Seminole Indians named the swamp "Land of the Trembling Earth."

Boardwalks allow you to walk over the prairies. Other attractions include observation towers, orientation films, exhibits, guided tours, nature trails, and boat rentals. Canoeing and primitive camping on raised platforms are popular pastimes.

Three entrances—at Folkston, Waycross, and Fargo— provide access to the swamp, recreational and educational opportunities, and accommodations.

The easiest entrance to reach from St. Marys is the east entrance at Folkston. From St. Marys, take State 40 west, then turn south for eleven miles on State 121/State 23. The Folkston entrance features the recreated Chesser Island Homestead, which demonstrates the self-sufficiency of pioneer swamp families. Tent and trailer accommodations can be found at Trader's Hill Recreation Park.

In the town of Folkston, the historic railroad depot, built in 1903, has been restored and houses the Folkston/Charlton County Chamber of Commerce as well as a museum of railroad artifacts.

The north entrance is near Waycross. From Folkston, take US 1/US 23 north. This section of the park includes a narrated boat ride, animal observation posts, a serpentarium, and a re-created pioneer homestead. The homestead, Obediah's Okefenoke, recreates the 1830s with reconstructed buildings and artifacts.

Nearby on North Augusta Avenue between US 1 and US 82 is the Okefenokee Heritage Center, filled with fine art and historical regional memorabilia. Southern Forest World, also on North Augusta Avenue, focuses on the logging and naval stores industries. Laura S. Walker State Park, 5653 Laura Walker Road, has tent and trailer sites, swimming, water-skiing, and fishing.

Historic downtown Waycross hosts the annual Pogofest in honor of the Okefenokee's most illustrious citizen, Pogo, of comic strip fame.

To reach Fargo on the west side of the swamp, take US 84 west from Waycross to Homerville, then US 441 south to Fargo. The Stephen C. Foster State Park, which abuts the west entrance, provides tent and trailer sites, cottages, a dock and ramp, fishing, trails, and a museum.

Once you've savored the attractions of Georgia's Colonial Coast, you'll agree that its slow pace and timeless appeal have been carefully preserved. We can only hope that it will endure. If you haven't already sampled Georgia's Golden Isles, you'll want to explore them next. In fact, you might combine both trails into one long trip.

In the Area

Brunswick-Golden Isles Local Welcome Center, I-95 between Exits 8 & 9, Brunswick, GA 31520, 912-264-0202 or 800-933-COAST.

Brunswick and Golden Isles Visitors Bureau, 4 Glynn Avenue at US 17, Brunswick, GA 31520, 912-265-0620.

Camden/Kings Bay Area Chamber of Commerce, P.O. Box 130, Kingsland, GA 31548, 912-729-5840.

Darien/McIntosh County Chamber of Commerce and Welcome Center, 105 Fort King George Drive (US 17 at Darien River Bridge), 912-437-4192 or 912-437-6684.

Darien/McIntosh County Welcome Center, I-95 at Exit 11, Eulonia, GA 31331, 912-832-4444, ext. 721.

Georgia Visitor Information Center at Kingsland/St. Marys, I-95, Kingsland, GA 31548, 912-729-3253.

Georgia Visitor Information Center, I-95, Garden City, GA 31418, 912-964-5094.

Richmond Hill/Bryan County Chamber of Commerce and Welcome Center, P.O. Box 1067, Richmond Hill, GA 31324, 912-756-2676.

St. Marys Tourism Council, 414 Osborne Street, St. Marys, GA 31558, 912-882-6200.

Savannah Area Convention and Visitors Bureau, 222 West Oglethorpe, Savannah, GA 31402, 912-944-0456.

Savannah Local Welcome Center (downtown), 301 Martin
    Luther King Boulevard, Savannah, GA 31401,
    912-944-0456 or 800-444-2427.

Waycross/Ware Tourism Bureau, 200 Lee Avenue, Waycross,
    GA 31502, 912-283-3742.

8 ~

Golden
Isles

Getting there: Take US 80 south from Savannah to Tybee Island.

Highlights: *Beaches, wildlife, forts, and lighthouses on four-teen barrier islands; horseback riding; birding; Jekyll Island's historic district; and an aquarium and museum of coastal history.*

Islas de oro—"islands of gold"—is the name the Spanish gave to what are now Georgia's Golden Isles. Had the English not defeated the Spanish in the 1742 Battle of Bloody Marsh on St. Simons Island, we might be speaking Spanish in Georgia today.

The Spanish didn't find the gold they were searching for, but they did find treasures—the coastal barrier islands. From north to south they are Tybee, Wilmington, Skidaway, Wassaw, Ossabaw, St. Catherines, Blackbeard, Sapelo, Wolf, Little St. Simons, St. Simons, Sea, Jekyll, and Cumberland Islands.

Georgia's "invisible Spanish heritage" was a Spanish mission system that was founded earlier than and lasted much longer than the mission system in the Southwest. In 1565, the Spanish had seventy Franciscan missionaries, serving 25,000 Indians at thirty-eight missions. However, there were many bloody confrontations between the Indians and the Spanish. When the Spanish retreated from the area, they left little that endured physically or culturally. In fact, no structure above ground survived. However, excavations on St. Catherines have revealed human remains, household items, weapons, and religious items such as rosaries and medallions.

Before the pyramids were built or Christianity began, there were Native American residents on St. Catherines. In 1526, a Spanish settlement was formed. In 1562, the French briefly claimed the islands and established a few forts. The English first ventured into the area in 1680, but the Spanish didn't retreat until 1686 and weren't completely expelled until 1742.

The real heritage of the Golden Isles is their natural beauty. You don't have to journey to the Caribbean, Hawaii, or even Florida to find golden—and often untouched—beaches, lush tropical vegetation, and exotic wildlife. History, recreation, and nature are all available off Georgia's coast. Instead of glitz, you'll find unpretentious diversions.

You won't even realize you're on an island as you cross heavily built up Wilmington Island on US 80. Separated from the mainland by the Intracoastal Waterway, it is between the waterway and Tybee Island and has no beaches.

Tybee Island, only fifteen minutes from Savannah via US 80, offers five miles of beach, as well as an amusement park, a water slide, and surf and charter-boat fishing. The island retains a 1950s ambience, with one-story motels, a variety of cottages, and small, casual mom-and-pop restaurants.

Hunter House Bed and Breakfast, 1701 Butler Avenue, offers accommodations and has a well-known restaurant.

Robert E. Lee's first assignment after his graduation from West Point was at Fort Pulaski, on Tybee Island. Designed by Napoleon's military engineer and built between 1829 and 1847, it was the pièce de résistance of brick and masonry forts. When the Confederates captured the fort in 1861, they thought they had an invincible obstruction of the Savannah River. However, bombardment by the Union's new rifled artillery in 1862 forced the Confederates to surrender in less than thirty hours. Later the fort was used as a Union military prison.

Fort Screven, also on Tybee Island, was built in 1875 and manned during the Spanish-American War and World Wars I and II. Relics and artifacts from precolonial days to World War II are displayed in a museum located in the bastioned vaults of the unrestored fort.

Upon founding Georgia, Gen. James Oglethorpe had a crude day marker built on the north end of Tybee Island as a navigation aid. A second tower was built in 1742; when lighted in 1748, it became the third lighthouse in America. The present 154-foot lighthouse was built in 1887. Guided tours are available. There is an adjacent museum with lighthouse artifacts.

The Marine Science Center on Tybee Island is an interpretive facility with aquariums and exhibits.

Skidaway Island, reached by State Loop 26, is primarily the home of upscale residential communities, country clubs, and golf courses. Skidaway Island State Park, also reached by State Loop 26, offers tent and trailer sites, a swimming pool, fishing, and hiking trails. The Skidaway Marine Science Complex and Aquarium conducts studies on area sea life and its potential uses. The aquarium exhibits Georgia marine life.

The following islands are accessible only by boat. Wassaw, Blackbeard, and Wolf Islands are national wildlife
refuges; Ossabaw Island is a heritage preserve. You can book
boat charters from Shellman Bluff or Pine Harbor. Sapelo
Island was the home of tobacco millionaire R. J. Reynolds.
Today it is a wildlife management area and the home of the
Sapelo Island Estuarine Research Reserve. Tours are available
at different times of the year from Meridian.

Little St. Simons Island is a 10,000-acre, privately owned
island with six miles of undeveloped beach. Access is only by
private ferry from St. Simons. A limited number of guests
(twenty-four) are accepted during certain periods of the year.
The staff includes two full-time naturalists and an intern, a
stable manager, fishing and boating guides, and an outstanding kitchen staff.

Wildlife is abundant in the maritime forests, including
more than 200 species of birds, making this island a popular
destination for naturalist groups such as the Audubon Society. Besides alligators, otters, and deer, you can see such
unusual creatures as armadillos. The island is one of the few
completely protected nesting grounds for sea turtles.

For the early bird, sunrise over the ocean is spectacular.
For lazy old folks like us, the sunsets over the marshes offer
some of the best picture taking we've ever enjoyed.

Horseback riding is offered early in the morning or late
in the afternoon. Canoeing, fishing, long walks, swimming
in the ocean or pool, kayak lessons, croquet, and boccie ball
tournaments provide other temptations. However, there's
nothing more relaxing than rocking on one of the porches
with a cocktail and a good book.

What we like about both Little St. Simons and Cumberland Island is that they provide one place we can just sit and
read a book without feeling guilty that we should be out un-
earthing other little-known sites or activities for our readers.

Most developed of all the barrier islands and reached by a causeway from Brunswick, St. Simons offers a look at the past as well as diverse modern leisure activities. The island was inhabited by Indians 4,000 years ago. The first Europeans were sixteenth-century Spanish monks from St. Augustine who built missions on what they called San Simon.

Later the English worked their way down the coast from Savannah. General James Oglethorpe built two forts, making St. Simons the southernmost English settlement in the New World. Settlers fared better here than those in Savannah because of the moderate climate and cooling sea breezes.

Visit Fort Frederica National Monument, where the remains of the fort and excavated foundations of the town that surrounded it offer glimpses of life in early Georgia.

The Wesley brothers, founders of Methodism, were among the first settlers. Christ Church, built in 1820 on a site where they preached, was destroyed during the Civil War. The present church replaced it in 1886. Superb stained-glass windows display scenes from the island's history. Several ghosts are said to haunt the graveyard.

At the southern tip of the island near the old village, city pier, and Neptune Park is the St. Simons Lighthouse and Museum of Coastal History. The original lighthouse was built in 1810, but it was destroyed by fleeing Confederate troops at the end of the Civil War. The present light was built in 1867. Still operating, it is one of the oldest continuously functioning lighthouses in the country. Visitors can climb the 129 steps to the top for a splendid panorama. The adjacent Victorian keeper's cottage houses the museum.

Legend has it that the pirate Bluebeard buried treasure on the island. Maybe you'll be the lucky one to find it.

A museum and former slave cabins are open to the public at Epworth-by-the-Sea, a Methodist retreat on what was Hamilton Plantation.

*St. Simons Lighthouse, where once the lighthouse keeper and his
assistant fought a duel to the death*

Long a vacation destination, St. Simons was popular with mainlanders from the 1880s, when visitors came from the mainland by train and ferry and were transported to and from the village by mule-drawn rail trolleys.

Although the rambling Victorian hotels of that day are long gone, St. Simons has a wide variety of accommodations. On the beach, the palatial King and Prince Resort offers golf, tennis, and sailing, as well as indoor and outdoor pools and a Jacuzzi. Lodging ranges from rooms in the main building to villas.

At Sea Palms you can stay in cottages or villas. In addition to tennis, the resort offers a golf course ranked among the top courses in Georgia.

Smaller motels, rental homes, cottages, and condominiums round out the choice of quarters. There are no campgrounds on St. Simons.

Across a small causeway from St. Simons is Sea Island. A residential enclave of the very rich, it is the site of the world-famous, five-star, five-diamond resort The Cloister. Since 1928, the Mediterranean-style resort has entertained presidents, potentates, honeymooners, and families one generation after another. The Cloister boasts a complete health spa, manicured golf courses, a beach club, skeet shooting, a racquet club, riding stables, fishing, sailing, and special weekends devoted to bridge, cooking, wine, dancing, and other pursuits.

Although Jekyll Island, reached by another causeway from the mainland, has ten miles of beaches, four golf courses including the state's largest, cable waterskiing, and an eleven-acre water park, the island is most famous for the Jekyll Island Club Historic Landmark District.

From 1886 to 1942, the island was privately owned by 100 millionaires—including a Goodyear, a Rockefeller, a Morgan, a Pulitzer, an Astor, and a Vanderbilt—for use as a retreat. A majestic, rambling Victorian clubhouse was built for communal activities, but each family built its own "cottage." We'd consider them mansions, but they had no kitchens because everyone ate at the club.

Unfortunately, World War II, the advent of modern transportation, and the fickleness of the rich and famous temporarily spelled doom for Jekyll Island as a vacation paradise, but in 1947 Jekyll Island was bought by the state. One of the most important benefits of state ownership is that building is severely restricted and the island has retained its charm. However, the prime result has been the massive restoration of the Millionaires District.

The project has become the largest restoration undertaking in the Southeast—240 acres and twenty-five buildings. As each house is restored, it is furnished with period antiques and art and opened to the public. The refreshed Jekyll Island Club was opened to the public as a Radisson hotel in 1988. Faith Chapel, with Tiffany stained-glass windows, is open at selected times. At the Orientation Center, located in the old stables, you can purchase tickets for a tram tour of the district with admission to several houses.

Other activities on Jekyll include the restored Tennis Center, used by the millionaires. It sports thirteen clay courts and a center court with grandstands. Sixty-three holes of golf are available. Joggers and bikers enjoy twenty miles of paths. From the wharf you can go on fishing trips, dolphin watches, and sunset cruises.

An eighteen-acre campground with 200 sites, rental cottages, villas, and condominiums are available. Several major hotel chains are represented, but none of them are in high-rises.

If you want to get away from commercialism and enjoy the simplicities of nature, try unique Cumberland Island—a national seashore protected in its primitive state. It can be reached only by a ferry run by the National Park Service from the mainland town of St. Marys. Only 300 visitors—including campers and day-trippers—per day are permitted.

Here on the largest of the Golden Isles, you'll find inland lakes and sixteen miles of pristine, deserted sea beaches backed by dunes and sea oats where birds and loggerhead turtles make their homes. Herds of wild horses graze in the meadows, marshes, and forest, and occasionally run on the beaches.

The entire island was once privately owned by the Carnegie family, who built several palatial mansions. One of these, thirty-room Plum Orchard, built in 1898, is being restored and is open for tours at selected times. Remains of their first home, Dungeness, can also be viewed, although it is not safe to walk among the ruins. A small Ice House Museum chronicles the island's history.

The aim of visiting Cumberland Island is to enjoy its natural, unspoiled beauty. This is a walking experience. No vehicles are permitted. Therefore, other than day visitors, most others are campers. Ferry and camping reservations are required. All supplies must be brought with you—there are no stores.

One accommodation does exist on Cumberland Island for the more comfort oriented. Elegant Greyfield Inn is a 1901 Carnegie mansion on 1,300 acres still controlled by the family. It has nine exquisite rooms, most with shared baths; three gourmet meals daily are included in the price. The inn operates its own private ferry from Fernandina Beach, Florida.

St. Simons, Jekyll, and Sea Island are often crowded in summer; autumn is a better time to visit. Air and water temperatures remain ideal while crowds have thinned. Even winter is popular for everything but swimming. At any time of year, reservations are strongly recommended.

You could take several vacations to the Golden Isles before seeing everything. You'll need to return again and again to do them justice. Conveniently, they're close enough to the mainland to visit on the spur of the moment. Do add some of the attractions on Georgia's mainland coast to your island itinerary, or come back again to see them.

In the Area

Brunswick-Golden Isles Convention and Visitors Bureau, 4 Glynn Avenue, Brunswick, GA 31520, 912-265-0620.

Cumberland Island, P.O. Box 806, St. Marys, GA 31558, 912-882-4336

Greyfield Inn, P.O. Box 900, Fernandina Beach, FL 32025-0900, 904-261-6408.

Jekyll Island Authority, 375 Riverview Drive, Jekyll Island, GA 31527, 912-635-2236.

Jekyll Island Convention and Visitors Bureau, One Beachview Drive, Jekyll Island, GA 31527, 912-635-4080 or 800-841-6586

Jekyll Island Local Welcome Center, 901 Jekyll Causeway, Jekyll Island, GA 31527, 912-635-3636 or 800-841-6586.

Little St. Simons Island Resort, P.O. Box 1078, Little St. Simons, GA 31522, 912-638-7472.

St. Simons and Sea Island Chamber of Commerce and Visitor Center, 530-B Beachview Drive, St. Simons, GA 31522, 912-638-9014.

Tybee Island Welcome Center, 200 Butler Avenue, Tybee Island, GA 31328, 912-786-5444.

9 ~

Mountain Magic

Getting there: Take State 348 from Helen.

Highlights: *Panning for gold; white-water rafting; waterfalls and covered bridges; fall foliage; spring azaleas, rhododendrons, and dogwood; Cabbage Patch kids; and the Old Sautee General Store.*

Where the earth meets the sky, fiery hues burn the mountainsides in the autumn. Spring bursts forth with blossoming azaleas, rhododendrons, mountain laurel, and dogwood. In the highest areas, summer breezes defeat the tyranny of summer heat. Tranquil snowfalls occasionally smooth rugged peaks in winter.

No matter what time of year, in the wilds of North Georgia, attractions are closely attuned to the outdoors. The mountains are a mecca for easygoing to strenuous outdoor activities set against a backdrop of unsurpassed beauty.

If you want to get away from people, traffic and airplane noises, and airborne and visual pollution, and enjoy birds singing, crickets chirping, and streams rippling (or roaring), and not spend big money doing it, the Northeast Georgia mountain region is the place to go. There is not a single large town in the region. The vast area is full of state parks and national forests, many with no admission charge.

Just driving around in North Georgia is entertaining enough. The scenery is spectacular—winding mountain roads enclosed by steep, forest-covered hillsides, placid lakes tucked into fertile valleys, torrents of water plunging into an abyss. You can go for miles without seeing a house, commercial establishment, or even a billboard. The most scenic drive is the Richard Russell Scenic Highway/State 348, which stretches 14.1 miles between State 180 (near Brasstown Bald) and State 75 at Helen.

Besides picnic and camping areas, Northeast Georgia's state parks have swimming areas and hiking trails. Some even offer paddle boats, minigolf, horseback riding, and other activities. The Appalachian Trail crosses US 19 several times.

If you crave a little more civilization, numerous small towns are filled with antique and craft shops as well as restaurants serving legendary home-style cooking. We'll concentrate on these small towns as we follow the 250-mile trail.

Dahlonega, which means "precious yellow metal" in Cherokee, is a good gateway for exploring the mountains. Long before the cry of "thar's gold in them thar hills" attracted prospectors to California, this country's first major gold rush occurred around what is now Dahlonega. After the forcible expulsion of the Cherokee, treasure seekers came by the thousands—drawn by the expectation of quick and easy fortunes. The influx of dreamers and schemers propelled the area into an era of booming prospecting and mining.

A U.S. mint was built west of town in 1837, making Dahlonega home to one of only seven official mints. Although the residents of Lumpkin County bucked Southern sentiment in 1861 by voting against secession from the Union, the area was forced to follow the rest of the state into the Confederacy. The federal government, therefore, ceased operation of the Dahlonega mint. It operated as a Confederate assay office during the Civil War, but was captured by the Union in 1865. Eventually the building burned, and what is now Price Memorial Hall of North Georgia College was built on the foundation. The gold-covered steeple rises above the building that serves as the college's administrative offices. Rare Dahlonega-minted coins are on display at the site of the old mint.

As most Georgians know, the dome of the state's capitol in Atlanta is gilded with gold leaf from Dahlonega. During the building's refurbishment several years ago, the gold was mined and refined in Dahlonega, then brought to Atlanta by wagon train, just as it had been when the dome was first decorated.

Although the major seams of gold have long been depleted, enough traces are left to provide entertainment and excitement for visitors. Several locations around town offer the opportunity to pan for gold.

Dahlonega is always bustling. The town is compactly arranged around a town square, in the center of which sits the Dahlonega Courthouse Gold Museum. Built in 1836 on the site of an original log cabin, it is the oldest public building in North Georgia and the second-most-visited historic site. The traditionally styled brick and white columned building began life as the county courthouse.

Inside are exhibits tracing the history of the county, gold-mining techniques, ore processing, and lifestyles of early residents. Visitors begin the tour on the second floor, still set up as a courtroom, with an audiovisual presentation.

But it's downstairs where tourists get gold fever. Of course, all the exhibits are well-protected by display cases and alarm systems, but the sight of gigantic blocks of shiny ore and piles of coins are awe inspiring. An immense old safe from that era shows how gold was protected before modern technology. Mining implements and enlarged historic photos line the walls. If you haven't already panned for gold before seeing the museum, you'll be ready to try your luck afterward.

Surrounding the square on all four sides are historic buildings—most erected before the turn of the century—brimming with restaurants and shops selling Appalachian crafts exemplifying and preserving mountain heritage. Don't miss The History Store—overflowing with books and maps of the area.

Get an idea what mining was like by touring Consolidated Mines, at US 19 and the State 60 Connector. Although the mine closed in the 1930s, it was the largest mining operation east of the Mississippi. You can also prospect for gold at Crisson's Mines at Goldminer's Camp.

Hidden away on a mountaintop just north of town on Wimpy Mill Road is a castle—yes, a castle—surrounded by vineyards. Cavender Castle operates as a winery and bed and breakfast. Even if you're not spending the night, you can enjoy the spectacular views, tour the operation, and finish up in the tasting room.

People drive from miles around to feast on home cooking served family style at The Smith House, just off the square at 202 South Chestatee Street, which also operates as a bed and breakfast. Other bed and breakfasts to choose from in or around Dahlonega are the Worley Homestead, 410 West Main Street; Miner's Deja Vu, 300 West Main Street; Royal Guard Inn, 203 South Park Street; and Mountain Top Lodge, Old Ellijay Road. Another alternative west of town is Forrest Hills

Mountain Hideaway—rated among the Top 50 Resorts in the country by *Lodging & Hospitality* magazine.

No matter what the season, you'll find golden moments in Dahlonega.

Before you leave town, pick up a brochure from the Welcome Center for "Dahlonega's Mountain Magic Trail—A Self-Guided Auto Tour," which guides you through the Chattahoochee National Forest for glimpses of picturesque lakes, secluded valleys, bubbling streams, and spectacular waterfalls—such as 729-foot Amicalola Falls.

Take US 19 north out of town and enjoy the spectacular scenery. You might want to stop at Helton Creek Falls. Then turn east onto US 129 to Cleveland—home of Babyland General Hospital, 19 Underwood Street, a fanciful world of make-believe where you can witness a "birth" and then adopt one of Xavier Roberts's original, soft-sculptured Cabbage Patch Kids. "Doctors and nurses" assist in the births and adoptions at the turn-of-the-century medical clinic.

Get information about the area from the White County Welcome Center, located in a 1901 jail building at 1700 North Main Street. The Old White County Courthouse, on the square, which was built between 1857 and 1859, houses the county historical society. Downtown Merchants Square brims with crafts, novelties, and food.

For luxury in the mountains, stay at Villagio di Montagna, on US 129, also owned by Xavier Roberts. Exquisite, individual, Spanish-style, tile-roofed villas are lavishly decorated with sleek, sophisticated Art Deco furnishings. Some units have fireplaces and/or spectacular bathroom/playrooms—some with oversized whirlpool tubs. Palazzo rooms in the lodge have balconies overlooking the river. An Olympic-sized pool, a hot tub, sauna, and steam room complete the amenities.

If you don't mind swarms of people and slow-moving traffic, you'll enjoy Helen, reached by heading north on State 75. About twenty-five years ago Helen was a small, dying logging town. Residents decided to try to save it by transforming it into a tourist attraction—a replica of a German, Swiss, or Austrian alpine village, complete with Bavarian facades on the buildings and narrow cobblestone alleys to explore. Shops feature European items and restaurants highlight European cuisine.

The idea may actually have been too good. Helen continues to grow unchecked. In addition to attractions such as a dinner theater and the Museum of the Hills in the center of town, dozens of motels, outlet malls, and tasting rooms from several of Georgia's wineries have mushroomed on the outskirts. Some kind of festival with entertainment is being celebrated practically all the time. In addition to Helen's famous Oktoberfest (which really lasts through September and October), Helen has special festivities at Christmas, as well as activities such as fasching, clogging, a St. Bernard show, hot-air balloon race, and canoe races throughout the year. The newest attraction is the Helenboch Brewery—Georgia's only microbrewery. All in all, traffic and parking can be a nightmare, especially during leaf season at the end of October.

A destination primarily for shoppers, Helen offers window-shopping, eating, and drinking—and people-watching if your purpose isn't spending a lot of money. Sitting at an open-air restaurant along a gurgling stream is remarkably soothing amidst the chaos. Pick up some information at the Helen Welcome Center in the City Hall building on Chattahoochee Street.

Leave Helen behind by traveling south on State 75 until you come to the Nora Mill Granary—a working gristmill built in 1876 on the banks of the Chattahoochee. You can purchase many wholesome freshly stone-ground grain mixes as well as grits and cornmeal.

Continue south on State 75 and step into another world—one of natural beauty and pioneer heritage. At the intersection of State 17 and State 75 is the Sautee-Nacoochee Indian Mound, built by ancient Native Americans thousands of years ago and much later reputed to be the resting place of tragic young lovers from warring Cherokee and Chickasaw tribes.

Turn east on State 17 and travel to Sautee. At the intersection of State 17 and State 255 is the Old Sautee General Store. The legendary emporium has stood at the junction of the Nacoochee and Sautee Valleys, in the center of what was once the Cherokee Nation, for 100 years. From the store, you can see the headwaters of the Chattahoochee River and lofty Mt. Yonah. Just as when it served the needs of pioneers, today the store museum displays an unusual collection of old-time merchandise. In addition, the store sells fine Scandinavian imports and Christmas merchandise.

Turn north on State 255 to the Sautee-Nacoochee Community Center, which operates as a history museum featuring memorabilia from the two valleys, as well as an art gallery and a performing arts hall.

Also on State 255 is the Stovall Covered Bridge. Built in 1895, it is the smallest covered bridge in the state. The highway has been rerouted around the bridge, but you can park and admire the king-post design and take pictures.

Several bed and breakfasts in the area offer simple to luxurious accommodations: Lumsden Homeplace, on Guy Palmer Road off State 255; Stovall House Country Inn and Restaurant, on State 255; and Nacoochee Valley Guest House and Restaurant and Grandpa's Room, on State 17. Another place to eat is the Sautee Inn Restaurant, located in a turn-of-the-century mountain inn on State 17 near the intersection with State 255.

Stop in at the Old Sautee Store, where a pair of cigar store Indians reminds you of a bygone era

Continue east on State 17 to Clarkesville, renowned for its mountain crafts and antique stores. "Goin' up to Clarkesville" has been a pastime of Georgians since the 1830s, when travelers came for the cool mountain air. The rehabilitated town square is filled with shops, galleries, and restaurants. One popular restaurant is Taylor's Trolley, located in a 1907 drugstore and soda fountain just off the square. Two bed and breakfasts right in town on Old US 441 offer accommodations and dining: the 1901 Victorian Burns-Sutton House and the 1907 Greek Revival Charm House.

North of town on State 197 is a famous family-style restaurant—LaPrade's. The complex, overlooking Lake Burton, also offers rustic cabins and a marina.

Return to Clarkesville and go north on Old US 441/US 23. (The new US 441 is a multilane, limited-access highway that bypasses Clarkesville and several other towns, but you want to stay on the old, scenic route.) Look for signs to the Glen-Ella Springs Hotel, on Bear Gap Road. Named one of *Travel & Leisure's* Top 10 Getaways, the completely restored rustic hostelry offers sixteen guest rooms and suites, spacious porches, a pool, gardens, and an award-winning restaurant.

Return to Old US 441/US 23, then detour east on State 17 to Toccoa. The Cherokee word for "beautiful," Toccoa is best known for 186-foot Toccoa Falls—a majestic lacelike veil of mist that cascades over a precipice 19 feet taller than Niagara Falls. Near the foot of the falls, which is on the grounds of Toccoa Falls College, is a gift shop and a restaurant that serves Sunday brunch.

When you first enter town, you'll see the highest point around—Currahee Mountain, which is Cherokee for "standing alone." In the center of town, you can get tourist information from Main Street Toccoa, 203 North Alexander Street. The historic walking tour encompasses shops, restaurants, and a museum. The Stephens County Historical Headquarters and Museum, located in an 1898 building at 313 South Pond Street, features memorabilia of famous local people, as well as artifacts of Native Americans, early settlers, and farmers.

Toccoa boasts two outstanding bed and breakfasts. The Habersham Manor House, 326 West Doyle Street, is in a restored 1906 Greek Revival mansion. The 1903 Simmons-Bond Inn, located in a Victorian house at 130 West Tugalo Street on the square, also has a restaurant.

East of town off US 123 is Traveler's Rest State Historic Site, a restored nineteenth-century stagecoach plantation house furnished with original trappings. Some famous overnighters included former U.S. vice president John C. Calhoun, and Joseph E. Brown, fiery Civil War governor of Georgia. Traveler's Rest features a ninety-foot-long porch, hand-numbered rafters, and twenty-inch-wide paneling.

Return to Old 441/US 23 and proceed north to Tallulah Gorge, detouring onto the scenic loop (watch for the signs) to observe one of the most significant geological features in the East. Created by the Tallulah River slicing through quartzite, the gorge is the oldest natural canyon in the country. At 1,200 feet deep, it is second in depth only to the Grand Canyon. The vast chasm was traversed on a tightrope in 1886 by a Professor Leon; the feat was repeated in 1970 by legendary circus performer Karl Wallenda.

From Tallulah Gorge Park, you can hike the half-mile trail along the ridge to an overlook, where you can observe Tempesta, Oceana, and Hurricane Falls. Although the Cherokee used the word for "terrible" to name the gorge because of the torrential flow of the river and pounding of the falls, today these cascades usually flow at only a fraction of their potential because the river is regulated by Georgia Power. Also in the park are the Old Town Museum and a gift shop.

There's another overlook across the highway at Terrora Park. Its visitors center features exhibits about the gorge and an interactive video about the Northeast Georgia mountains.

On US 441/US 23 between Tallulah Falls and Clayton is the Hambridge Center. Established in 1934, it is a community center for the arts. Programs include weaving, pottery, dance, music, nature, creative writing, photography, painting, and art history. In Tiger, off US 441, is the Four Winds Indian Museum and Trading Post, which features antiques, pottery, crafts, and gems. Also on US 441, Lofty Branch is an artists' compound featuring many mountain craftspeople whose studios are open to the public. Twice a year, in May and October, Lofty Branch sponsors an arts and crafts fair called Mountain Maffick. Maffick means "to celebrate with boisterous rejoicing and hilarious behavior."

At Lake Rabun, you can enjoy the rustic 1922 Lake Rabun Hotel.

Clayton, farther north on US 441/US 23, is a center for white-water rafting and other outdoor pursuits. Stop at the Rabun County Local Welcome Center on US 441 for information. Rabun County is wild river country. The Chattooga River, famous for its spectacular scenery and thrilling rapids, is designated as a National Wild and Scenic River. The lower portions of the river provide outstanding rafting and canoeing in what is considered one of the last true wilderness areas in the East.

A fascinating place to stay near Clayton is English Manor Inns, on US 76. Although the bed and breakfast began life as a simple 1912 Sears kit house, it has mushroomed into five buildings and eighty rooms and suites—all different. Two popular restaurants are The Stockton House, which overlooks Warwoman Dell and Mountain, and Green Shutters, famous for its open-hearth specialties.

Once upon a time, the Tallulah Falls Railroad brought visitors to Mountain City, north of Clayton on US 441/US 23, for vacations in the cool mountains. Vacationers stayed in comfortable old inns such as the York House, which has been serving as a country hotel since the turn of the century.

The square-dancing barn is gone, as is the Mountain City Playhouse; today Mountain City is known for Foxfire books, about the lives and skills of mountain people in Rabun County. You can examine artifacts from the series at the Foxfire Press and Museum, on US 441.

Continue north on US 441 to Dillard—famous for the Dillard House, a world-renowned family-style restaurant featuring items the Dillard family grows in the fertile valley they've been farming since the Revolutionary War. In addition to the restaurant, the Dillards offer a self-contained resort with elegant suites and cozy cottages, a petting zoo, horseback riding, tennis, and swimming.

For those of us who rarely see snow, a trip to Sky Valley Resort, at the extreme northeast corner of the state, during winter can be a special treat. Where else can you ski while watching those lower down the mountain playing golf? Georgia's only ski resort, Sky Valley is the southernmost ski slope in the United States. Chalets hug the mountainside directly on the ski slopes, but you also can choose from cabins, condominiums, or single homes. A winter getaway might involve skiing all day, dining in the cozy lodge, followed by après-ski activities in the rustic lounge, then back to your cabin to laze by the glow of your fireplace. With 2,400 acres bordered by national forest, the retreat seems boundless. Billed as a "Resort for All Seasons," it offers golf, tennis, swimming, horseback riding, and other sports. To reach Sky Valley, turn east on State 246 at Dillard, then follow the signs to the resort.

Return to Clayton and turn west on US 76 to Hiawassee. The Indian name for "pretty fawn," Hiawassee abounds with Native American legends. On US 76 overlooking Lake Chatuge is the most famous fair in the state—the Georgia Mountain Fair—which runs for three weeks in August and offers crafts, entertainment, and lots of fabulous southern food. Part of the fair is a Pioneer Village, where Appalachian heritage is recreated in a mountain town setting with demonstrations of old-fashioned techniques of board splitting, moonshining, quilting, soapmaking, and more.

Located within the grounds of the Georgia Mountain Fair, the Fred Hamilton Rhododendron Gardens display more than 2,000 varieties of rhododendrons and azaleas.

During the summer, Georgia's official state play, "The Reach of Song," is performed in Hiawassee. The epic historical drama, as seen through the life and work of native poet Byron Herbert Reece, is filled with regional music, dance, and humor.

Completely hidden in secluded Hickory Nut Cove, overlooking a perfect lake, is Swan Lake B&B.

Continue west on US 76 to Blairsville, where the 1898 courthouse houses a historical museum. A "mustn't miss" item on any trip to North Georgia is Brasstown Bald, the highest mountain peak in Georgia, at nearly 4,800 feet above sea level. From the top you'll have a panorama of four states. To reach Brasstown Bald from Blairsville, go south on US 129, then east on State 180. Signs will direct you to the mountain.

Return to US 129 and go south to Neel's Gap atop Blood Mountain, the second-highest mountain in Union County. Archaeologically rich in Native American history, the mountain was named for the blood spilled during battles between Creeks and Cherokees. The Appalachian Trail crosses the highway here. Continue south on US 129/US 19 and you'll arrive back in Dahlonega.

Alternatives for the long route we chose are two shorter self-guided driving tours available from the North Georgia Mountains Travel Association, P.O. Box 464, Gainesville, GA 30503. One tour explores the area west of Helen and the other the area east of Helen.

In North Georgia, fairs are held throughout the year with crafts, folk-art demonstrations, folk stories, singing, foods, and other attractions.

For those who want to stay over in North Georgia, the region has the state's largest concentration of bed and breakfasts. You can camp for $5.00 per night in the state parks, some of which also have cabins for rent. Unicoi and Amicalola Falls State Parks each have a lodge as well as campsites and cabins. Small, old motels and cabins can be found everywhere and can be quite inexpensive. Newer midpriced motels and cabins are also available in most towns, and several new luxury properties have been opened.

You might guess that the North Georgia mountain region is one of our favorite Georgia destinations. Maybe it's because the mountains, vegetation, wildlife, crafts, activities, and foods remind us so much of our childhood homes in western Maryland and western Pennsylvania.

In the Area

Dahlonega/Lumpkin County Chamber of Commerce/ Welcome Center, 101 South Park Street, Dahlonega, GA 30533, 706-864-3711.

Rabun County Chamber of Commerce and Convention and Visitors Bureau, P.O. Box 750, Clayton, GA 30525, 706-782-4812.

Toccoa-Stephens County Chamber of Commerce/Local Welcome Center, 907 East Currahee Street, Toccoa, GA 30577, 706-886-2132.

Towns County Chamber of Commerce, US 76, The Hamlet 4, Hiawassee, GA 30546, 706-896-4966.

White County Chamber of Commerce, 1700 North Main Street, Cleveland, GA 30528, 706-865-5356.

10 ~

Peach Blossom Trail

Getting there: Take US 41, US 341, or US 23 from Jonesboro.

Highlights: Gone With the Wind *plantations and memorabilia, Georgia peaches, camellias, an aviation museum, and the Whistle Stop Cafe.*

Moonlight and magnolias—this is truly *Gone With the Wind* country. Those visitors on the trail of Scarlett O'Hara will be happy to know that much of Margaret Mitchell's inspiration came from this area. When she was a child, her family would ride by carriage from Atlanta to her grandparents' country home in Clayton County. Years later, she drew on her memories not only of the places and homes she visited, but also of the courage and strong-mindedness of the people who had endured both the Civil War and Reconstruction—the citizens whose world was "gone with the wind."

During the creation of her novel, Mitchell did a lot of her research at Jonesboro's 1898 courthouse. But what about Tara and Twelve Oaks—where are they? In the South, many antebellum homes are rumored to have been one or the other, but in truth the two estates existed only in Mitchell's imagination and as facades on a back lot in Hollywood. She may have combined elements of several Clayton homes to create her fictional world. Whether or not a particular estate figured in her descriptions, it's fun to visit many of the graceful surviving homes and picture Scarlett sweeping down the staircase or Rhett lounging against a porch column.

The Peach Blossom Trail, through central Georgia, is where the Confederacy meets the New South. It offers the visitor a potpourri of pleasures evocative of sun-blushed peaches. Spring is a visual feast of peach trees bedecked in pink and white blossoms. In summer, you can pick your own fuzzy delicacies, and there's no shortage of peach-inspired dishes—cobbler, ice cream, jams, preserves, and wines. Civil War history is leavened with tidbits of ancient Indian lore. A mélange of peaches, people, and places, the trail ambles 200 miles in a loop along US 41, US 341, and US 23, with Jonesboro as the gateway in the north and Perry in the south.

We'll explore the route from the north, beginning in Jonesboro, just south of metro Atlanta off US 41 and State 138. At the end of the long, brutal summer of 1864, the Battle of Jonesboro marked the beginning of the end in the Atlanta Campaign. Although the Battle of Atlanta had raged for weeks, Gen. William Tecumseh Sherman's federal troops were still unable to conquer the Confederacy's railroad transportation center.

So Sherman instead severed Jonesboro's rail lines, which kept the entrenched Confederates well supplied, during a two-day battle along Main Street in Jonesboro on August 31 and September 1, 1864. Cut off from being resupplied from the south, Confederate troops in Atlanta were forced to surrender and evacuate.

Get a Historic Jonesboro Driving Tour brochure from the Visitors Bureau at 8712 Tara Boulevard (US 41/US 19). The tour includes thirty significant heritage properties.

Begin with the 1867 Depot, 104 North Main Street. Constructed from blue and gray Georgia granite, this depot replaces the one burned by Sherman's troops. It still contains old cotton and baggage scales, as well as Tara Relics, a shop that sells Civil War and *Gone With the Wind* memorabilia.

The buildings in the old business district were burned by Union troops in 1864, but only the interiors were destroyed. Refurbished, many retain their antebellum appearance. Gone, however, are the five raucous saloons that used to occupy the basements of these buildings.

Ashley Oaks Mansion is an elegantly furnished 1879 Italianate town house located at 144 College Street. Two-story Ashley Oaks was the second brick residence in Clayton County. The construction of its solid brick interior and exterior walls required more than a million bricks and resulted in walls more than twenty-four inches thick. The sumptuous furnishings include Waterford and Baccarat crystal chandeliers and a collection of Madame Alexander Scarlett dolls.

Stately Oaks Plantation Home and Historic Community, headquarters of Historical Jonesboro, is an 1839 dwelling and outbuildings on the edge of town at 100 Carriage Lane. Scattered about the grounds of the Greek Revival mansion are an original log kitchen, a one-room schoolhouse, an old country store, and formal colonial gardens.

Patrick R. Cleburne was a Confederate general who won a major battle at Pickett's Mill (see Blue and Gray Trail). He then commanded the Southern forces at the Battle of Jonesboro. He was killed later in the war at Franklin, Tennessee. A monument in the Pat Cleburne Confederate Memorial

Cemetery, at Johnson and McDonough Streets, honors him and Confederate dead who fell in the Battle of Jonesboro.

The Warren House, 102 West Mimosa Drive, was used as a hospital first by the South and then by the Union. Signatures of Northern soldiers can still be seen on the walls. An interesting sidelight to the Johnson-Blalock House, 155 North Main Street, is that the woman who lived there during the Civil War was Martha Holliday Johnson, aunt of the infamous Doc Holliday. The house was used as a storehouse for Confederate supplies and later as a hospital.

Return to US 41/US 19 and go south. Along the highway, look on the right for the Sigma Chi Cross, a 100-ton Georgia Cherokee marble monument commemorating the Constantine Chapter of Sigma Chi, formed here on the night of September 17, 1864, by seven young Confederate soldiers who had been members of the fraternity at several southern universities before the war.

Look for Talmadge Road and turn right. You can drive by the private Crawford-Talmadge Plantation, now known as Lovejoy Plantation. The handsome Greek Revival structure, built in 1835, sits back from the road on sweeping lawns. Reputed to have inspired Twelve Oaks, it was the site where Confederate Gen. John Bell Hood assembled his army after the fall of Atlanta. The house is open only for previously arranged group tours.

On US 41/US 19 just north of the junction with State 20 is the Atlanta Motor Speedway, where you can watch two NASCAR Winston Cup races, the Busch Grand National, and IMSA and SCCA auto racing events from March through November.

Just south of the speedway, turn east on State 20 to historic Hampton. The attractive Train Depot on Main Street, built in 1881 of fireproof brick with ornate brick detailing, served not only as a passenger terminal but also as a cotton warehouse. Today, the depot houses city offices. Like many railroad towns of the Victorian period, Hampton is filled with beautiful homes, especially those lining the tracks on North Main Street, East Main Street, and Oak Street.

Drive by Oakleigh Manor, on Wynne Road. Built in 1860, the home was rumored to be Sherman's headquarters and to have been spared because of its Masonic emblem.

Return to US 41/US 19 and continue south to Milner. The Confederate Cemetery on Old Alabama Road was the burial site of more than 100 Confederate troops, most of whom were killed in the Battle of Atlanta.

Continue south on US 41/US 19 to Barnesville. Barnesville Hardware, 116 Main Street, built in 1870 in Gothic Revival style, was formerly the showroom of the Smith Buggy Company—one of four buggy manufacturers that made Barnesville "the buggy capital of the world." It is one of the oldest operating hardware stores in the state. Get a brochure for a walking tour of the downtown area and Victorian homes from the Chamber of Commerce, 109 Forsyth Street.

The Confederate Cemetery, on Greenwood Street, contains 150 Confederate graves, including that of "Uncle" George Schram, a Confederate veteran who walked to all the Confederate reunions until he was in his eighties.

Take US 341 south to Culloden, which was the site of a famous Civil War battle. On April 19, 1865—just days after Lee's surrender to Grant at Appomattox and the assassination of Abraham Lincoln—only 200 men of the Confederate Worrill Grays held off a much larger force of Union troops. The Confederate Museum, on Main Street, contains a small collection of memorabilia.

The Historic Methodist Church is the oldest Methodist Church in Georgia in continuous use. The grave of the town's founder, William Culloden, is in the town cemetery behind the church.

Continue south on US 341 to Musella. Dickey's Peach Packing Shed, on Old State 341, has been in continuous operation since 1890. The Musella Cotton Gin, also on Old State 341, was built in 1913. It is the only operational gin of its kind in a fifty-mile radius.

Turn off US 341 at Roberta and go east on US 80 to Knoxville—the birthplace of John Pemberton, creator of the Coca-Cola formula. The Courthouse, rebuilt in 1851, is the oldest Georgia courthouse in continuous use. The 1834 Old Knoxville Jail and Museum contains memorabilia, documents, and local history.

Return to Roberta on US 341. The downtown historic district, incorporated in 1910, includes the restored Georgia Post Building and a vintage general store. The Benjamin Hawkins monument is located downtown. The Benjamin Hawkins gravesite is off State 128.

The pre-1835 Pope Place, on Avery Road, was the home of Joanna Troutman, who designed the Texas Lone Star Flag for Georgians to carry to Texas in their volunteer fight to help Texans win their independence from Mexico. Her bedroom is preserved as it was originally furnished.

Continue south on US 341 to Fort Valley, county seat of Peach County and site of June's Peach Festival. In Peach County, four packing plants offer retail shopping and tours. One of those is Lane Packing Company, on State 96 east. Visitors can view the entire peach-packing process from an elevated platform overlooking the football field–sized plant. This four-generation family operation packs more than thirty varieties of peaches, handpicked by about 400 workers. More than 300,000 peaches per hour are individually weighed, counted, separated, and packed. This is the only plant of its kind in the East, using computer-controlled equipment and soft-handling techniques. Visit the roadside market and gift shop, and be sure to sample homemade peach ice cream or peach or blackberry cobbler.

In addition to peaches, pecans are an important Georgia product. Since 1924, the Jolly Nut Company has sold pecans in many forms. Located next to the processing plant, at 114 Commercial Drive, the Pecan Store offers gifts from Georgia, candy, antiques, and recipes.

The Blue Bird Body Company is an attraction of a different sort. Blue Bird—the largest manufacturer of school buses in the world—is open for tours by prior arrangement. The company also creates the Wanderlodge, an exclusive luxury recreational vehicle.

Between Fort Valley and Marshallville on State 49 is the headquarters of the American Camellia Society at Massee Lane Gardens. Their nine-acre garden is home to many species of the fragrant and colorful flower. Camellias bloom November through March; other plants flower throughout the year. Begin with a slide presentation giving you the history of camellias and the society.

An authentic Japanese garden, an extensive library, a gift shop, and an impressive collection of Boehm porcelains, rivaling those of Mobile's Bellingrath Gardens, are additional attractions. The Boehm porcelains and other objets d'art are displayed in the Stevens-Taylor Gallery and the Fetterman Museum.

The excellent place to stay in Fort Valley is the Evans-Cantrell House B&B, 300 College Street, an Italian Renaissance Revival mansion built in 1916 by A. J. Evans, well-known as "The Peach King" because of his numerous orchards and packing operations.

Continue south on US 341 to Perry. Known as the "crossroads of Georgia" because of its position at the geographic center of the state, where US 341, US 41, and the Golden Isles Parkway intersect with I-75, Perry was named after naval hero Commodore Oliver Hazard Perry and is the northern starting point of the Andersonville Trail and a site on the Antiques Trail (see those chapters).

From the Perry Welcome Center, at 101 Courtney Hodges Boulevard just off I-75, you can get a brochure for a historic walking/driving tour.

At Cranshaw's One Horse Farm and Day Lily Gardens, on US 41, you can picnic on twenty-five acres among 1,000 varieties of day lilies that bloom in May and June.

There's always something going on in Perry. The Georgia National Fairgrounds and Agricenter, a mammoth exhibition facility just off I-75 at US 41, is the home of the Georgia National Fair each October, as well as horse shows, stock shows, and rodeos throughout the year. The Southeastern Antiques and Collectibles Market is held there the fourth weekend of each month.

On the third weekend of April and October, the Mossy Creek Barnyard Festival, on State 96, provides an opportunity to glimpse "The Way It Used To Be." In addition to pioneer demonstrations, music and food enhance the celebration.

Christmas at the Crossroads is a month of old-fashioned Christmas celebrations and events. The Garden Tour in March is when residents open up their backyards so visitors can enjoy the flowers.

Peach picking is a major activity around Perry. Several orchards invite you to pick your own, or you can buy fresh peaches from roadside stands from mid-May to mid-August.

Go north out of Perry on US 41, then turn east on State 247C to Warner Robins. A small town of just fifty residents in 1940, Warner Robins has become Georgia's fastest-growing city—already the state's sixth largest. World War II brought this transformation as the Robins Army Air Depot became an air force base and a major logistics and avionics center.

A celebration of man's fascination with flight, the Museum of Aviation at Robins Air Force Base, 1420 Watson Boulevard/State 247C, is the fastest-growing air museum in the Southeast. Only ten years old, the 102,000-square-foot exhibition building on forty-five acres features more than eighty historic aircraft, as well as a major collection of aviation memorabilia dating back to World War I. Flight enthusiasts will enjoy three floors of dioramas, hands-on displays including flight simulators and laser light gunnery turrets, and a technical-historical research center. A special wing dedicated to Georgia's aviators is the Georgia Aviation Hall of Fame.

An annual highlight is the two-day Robins Air Force Base Open House Air Show in October. Military and civilian aircraft are displayed, and there are team and solo air performances.

Retrace State 247C past US 41 and go north on I-75 one exit to Byron—the picture of quiet southern charm. Incorporated in 1874, Byron owes its birthright to the railroads and to peaches. The Byron Museum, in the 1870 depot, showcases both facets of Byron's heritage with memorabilia, photographs, and furniture of the glamorous bygone days. Handsome Victorian and Neoclassical turn-of-the-century residences line the railroad tracks. Byron pays homage to the importance of peaches with the Big Peach Monument.

Continue north on I-75 through Macon and turn north on US 23. Whether or not you've seen the movie *Fried Green Tomatoes*, you'll enjoy a visit to tiny Juliette, where it was filmed. In its heyday, Juliette was a bustling textile and railroad town—its mill was once the world's largest powered by water. However, when the mill closed in 1957, the town began to die. The stores were boarded up, the houses were abandoned, and the mill deteriorated. All that changed overnight when the town was discovered as a movie site in 1991.

Even knowing that the town had been rediscovered, we weren't prepared for how popular it is. Imagine our surprise when, after driving miles on deserted country roads, we reached minuscule Juliette on a weekday to find a traffic jam and swarms of people clogging the streets. "They must be having a festival," I said. But, no, this was just a normal day.

Literally a country crossroads, this picturesque hamlet centers around the famous Whistle Stop Cafe, on McCrackin Street, where you can indeed step back fifty years and enjoy those fried green tomatoes, as well as other southern specialties. The cafe is open from 8:00 A.M. to 2:00 P.M. daily, noon to 7:00 P.M. on Sundays, but be forewarned: it's on a first-come, first-served basis, and the lines are long. Just sign your name on the list hanging on the screen door. We were too late to get in line before the cut-off time. A fortunate few can while away their wait in one of several rocking chairs on the porch.

Other historic buildings, including the bank, courthouse, depot, drugstore, and old dry-goods stores, now house quaint boutiques such as Towanda's, antique shops, and food outlets. Stop in at the tiny wooden courthouse, where the honorary mayor will regale you with Juliette's history. Be sure to sign the guest book. On the day we visited, tourists from Germany, the Netherlands, England, and Canada had preceded us.

You'll recognize other sites from the movie: the old deserted gristmill sitting forlornly along the railroad tracks, and the dam and headgates of the Ocmulgee River, which provided the power for the mill. Juliette was a victim of Georgia's catastrophic July 1994 floods, but it's been cleaned up and is back in business.

Leaving Juliette, turn right off McCrackin Street onto Juliette Road, go four miles, and turn right again. Follow the signs 3.5 miles—part on gravel road, most on dirt road—to Jarrell Plantation Historic Site. Operated by the State Parks Department, the site depicts farm life from the 1840s to the 1940s. Although such a compound is called a plantation because it is a self-contained, self-sufficient world, this is not the romantic, white-columned plantation of *Gone With the Wind*. The farm includes twenty historic buildings, including several original rustic homes, farm buildings, a cotton gin, and a sawmill. Many engines and tools are displayed. Farm animals, gardens, and a grape arbor lend an air of authenticity.

Successive generations of the Jarrell family made their home here for 100 years, withstanding wars, economic depression, soil erosion, and boll weevils. The buildings and artifacts they willed to the state make up one of the largest and most complete collections of original family artifacts in Georgia. You'll be fascinated by the carpenter shop, blacksmith shop, three-story barn, beehives, well, shingle mill, cane furnace, cane mill and planer, smokehouses, and wheat houses.

Borrow a guide brochure from the Visitors Center, which offers an audiovisual orientation describing the Jarrell family and the history of the farm. Special events and exhibits are held throughout the year.

Return to US 23 and go north to Indian Springs, which got its name from a medicinal spring. The historic Indian Spring Hotel, on US 23, was built in 1823 by Chief William McIntosh, leader of the Lower Creek Nation (see the Chieftans Trail). The hotel is surrounded by an authentic 1800s rose and herb garden. Operated as a museum, the hotel is open Sundays from May through October. Across US 23 is Indian Springs State Park, the oldest state park in the nation.

Proceed north on US 23 to the tiny hamlet of Locust Grove. Named for the flowering locust trees that grow there, it is the home of Noah's Ark—a rehabilitation center that provides temporary or permanent housing and care for injured and orphaned animals. At any one time, the facility may shelter more than 600 animals.

Continue north on US 23 to McDonough. The Courthouse, built in 1897, contains the Jail Museum. Also on the Courthouse Square is the Old Post Office. Completed in 1940 as a public works project, it features murals telling the story of cotton in the South by French artist Jean Charlot, who later became art director of the Guggenheim Museum in New York City. A walking tour brochure is available at the Chamber of Commerce, at 1310 State 20 west.

To get back to Perry, return to US 23 and go north. On your journey, we hope you savored all the history as well as some fresh peaches, and have brought home not only peaches, but plenty of pecans, and lots of new recipes to try.

In the Area

Clayton County Local Welcome Center, 8712 Tara
  Boulevard, Jonesboro, GA 30237, 404-478-6549.

Barnesville-Lamar County Chamber of Commerce, 109
  Forsyth Street, Barnesville, GA 30204, 404-358-2732.

Henry County Chamber of Commerce/Convention and
  Visitors Bureau, 1310 State 20 West, McDonough, GA
  30253, 404-957-5786.

Peach County Chamber of Commerce, 114 Vineville Street,
  Ft. Valley, GA 31030, 912-825-3733.

Perry Area Chamber of Commerce, 1105 Washington Street, Perry, GA 31069, 912-987-1234.

Perry Area Convention and Visitors Bureau/Welcome Center, 101 General Courtney Hodges Boulevard, Perry, GA 31069, 912-988-8000.

Warner Robins Tourism Division, 1420 Watson Boulevard, Warner Robins, GA 31093, 912-922-8585.

11 ~

Plantation Trace

Getting there: Take US 84 or US 27 at Bainbridge.

Highlights: *Pebble Hill Plantation—the state's finest, African art, sand dunes, a Native American festival, an agricultural heritage center, and roses.*

Americans maintain an endless love affair with the romantic and opulent days that preceded the Civil War—fueled by the timeless popularity of *Gone With the Wind* and the PBS special *The Civil War*. Visitors want to find Tara—which never existed. However, in the rolling red clay hills of southwest Georgia, you can find America's largest enduring collection of plantations. What's more, most of these seventy-one manors are still working estates, although many of them are open to the public only during special events.

This area is known as Georgia's Plantation Trace—not only for the plantations but for the many interesting paths or routes there are to explore. This 200-mile trail also has other attractions, sporting and hunting possibilities, and Indian heritage.

Native Americans first lived on this land of bountiful woodlands and waters, followed by frontier soldiers. In 1675, the Spanish bishop of Cuba established a mission called Sabacola. Then farmers came to till the fertile agricultural plains. Timber barons exploited the forests. But it wasn't until the 1880s that the region began to flourish when northerners discovered the area's mild winter climate and pine-scented air, which they believed had therapeutic properties. In addition, the area was free of the lowland marshes that bred yellow fever– and malaria-carrying mosquitoes. Sportsmen found an abundance of quail and other game. Soon fine hotels emerged, and wealthy industrialists built grand town homes or vast estates.

Bainbridge, located in the western part of the region at US 84 and US 27, began life as an Indian trading post along the Flint River. When prosperity hit town, a frenzy of building resulted in neighborhoods, such as that around Willis Park, characterized by stately Victorian and Neoclassical homes. Explore these neighborhoods by getting a brochure for a self-guided Bainbridge Heritage Tour from the Chamber of Commerce and Visitor Information Center, located in the McKenzie-Reynolds House at the Earl May Boat Basin Park, West Shotwell Street. A 600-acre site, the marina offers boat docks, fishing, baseball, tennis, a playground, and the Steam Engine Museum.

Once you have your guide, the historic driving tour highlights fifty sites that are turn of the century or earlier. The Steamboat House, 206 East Evans Street, is a Neoclassical Revival home built by a riverboat fleet owner. Willis Park, downtown, is an oasis with a restored Victorian gazebo and a fish pond set amidst lush landscaping. The White House Bed and Breakfast is in one of the restored antebellum homes.

More water sports are available at Lake Seminole, with fishing being a particularly popular pastime. Jack Wingate's Bass Island Campground and Lunker Lodge is famous for its unpretentious atmosphere and the fresh fish served at the restaurant. The Gopher Tortoise Nature Trail, at Seminole State Park, meanders through the habitat of Georgia's only native tortoise.

From Bainbridge, take US 27 north to Colquitt. Known as "The Mayhaw Jelly Capital," the town has a yearly Mayhaw Festival where you can watch how the jelly and other mayhaw products are made from the cranberry-sized fruit found in swamps and bogs. All the products are for sale, of course.

Take State 91 north to Albany, largest city in the Plantation Trace. Downtown, the Thronateeska Heritage Foundation focuses on both the Native American and European cultures and the natural history of Southwest Georgia. Its Thronateeska Heritage Museum of History and Science, located in a historic railroad depot at Heritage Plaza, 100 Roosevelt Avenue, displays a collection of Indian artifacts and shells, antique carriages and automobiles, miniature trains, changing historical exhibits, and the Wetherbee Planetarium.

Visit St. Teresa's Catholic Church, which served as a Civil War hospital; the 1860 Smith House; and the Community Theater, housed in the 1860s Brinson-Davis House.

The Albany Museum of Art, 311 Meadowlark Drive, houses the largest collection of African art in the Southeast. The museum also contains a permanent collection of nineteenth- and twentieth-century American and European art.

One of the Seven Wonders of Georgia is Radium Springs, at 2500 Radium Springs Road, the largest natural spring in Georgia. Water in the sandy beach–edged summer swimming spot is always sixty-eight degrees. The 1920s casino has been converted into a restaurant.

Although not listed as one of the Seven Wonders, we think the Sand Dunes on East Oglethorpe Boulevard deserve to be added. According to some geological experts, one million years ago these fossil dunes were at the northern edge of the Gulf of Mexico—now more than 100 miles away. The dunes extend thirty miles along the Flint River and peak at Albany.

Chehaw Park, on Philema Road (State 91), is a 700-acre preserve with campgrounds, play areas, jogging, bicycle, and hiking trails. The centerpiece of the park is the Chehaw Wild Animal Park, where animals roam freely in their native habitat while human visitors watch from trails and elevated walkways. The park also includes a petting zoo, Civilian Conservation Corps log cabins, and a gift shop. The Chehaw National Indian Festival, held at the park each May, is a major Indian cultural event with dancing, storytelling, and crafts.

From Albany, take US 82 east to Tifton, where 70 percent of the downtown buildings are on the National Register of Historic Places. A turn-of-the-century hotel at 128 First Street, once the finest hotel south of Atlanta, has been reborn and now contains restaurants, shops, businesses, and the Myon Bed and Breakfast. One of our favorite restored buildings is the Art Deco Tift Theater, where cultural events are held throughout the year. The town also has several art galleries, one in an old railroad depot.

Tifton, named one of the 100 Best Small Towns in America, is the site of one of our favorite festivals—A Love Affair. The annual arts celebration gets its name two ways: some of the major events occur on Love Avenue, and "everyone loves a fair."

You can explore Georgia's small-town past at the Agrirama, Georgia's Agricultural Heritage Center. Using thirty-five historic buildings moved to the site from around Georgia, a living-history rural town has been recreated. The town includes an industrial complex and farmsteading communities of the 1870s and 1890s. Agrirama hosts several yearly events: Country Fair of 1896 in May, cane-grinding parties in November, and the Wiregrass Opry each Saturday evening from April through October.

Out in the country, north of Tifton, is Hummingbird's Perch, a bed and breakfast named for the multitudinous little powerhouses that come to feast in the perfumed gardens. A small lake and walking trails allow you to commune with nature in peace and quiet.

From Tifton, take US 319 south to Moultrie. Knowing that the Plantation Trace is quail country, the more adventurous traveler might like to try his or her hand at one of several quail-hunting plantations such as Pinefields Plantation.

Historic downtown Moultrie has an array of interesting buildings. The Colquitt County Arts Center, 401 Seventh Avenue, is the center of permanent and touring art exhibits as well as performing arts. At the Ellen Payne Odom Genealogy Library, 204 Fifth Street, information is available for the entire eastern seaboard and migration routes west, and includes archives of major Scottish clans. At the Moultrie Olympic Quality Diving Facility, national and international meets are held throughout the diving season.

In October, Moultrie is abuzz with the Sunbelt Agricultural Exposition, the largest farm show in the Southeast. Activities include crop and equipment demonstrations, exhibits, food, and entertainment. Colquitt County is recognized for producing the greatest variety of fruits and vegetables in the state.

Continue south on US 319 to Thomasville, the Rose City. The town was chartered in 1831 and enjoyed a gilded age as a premier winter resort for thirty years around the turn of the century, when wealthy northerners traveled here by rail to take advantage of the moderate climate. Its elegant hotels were visited by presidents, royalty, business tycoons, and famous actors. Several of the rich and famous tourists liked the area so well that they built seasonal "cottages." Many of these mansions are still owned by family descendants, and some are open for public tours.

Although the grand hotels are long gone, and many of the tourists have moved on to more exotic locations, the town contains numerous remnants of those golden days. There are seven official historic districts, and it is said that every form of architecture is represented in the nineteenth-century buildings. Guided historic tours, some of which include outlying plantations, depart from the Welcome Center, 401 South Broad Street, where you can also get a brochure for a self-guided tour of thirty-six sites.

The Queen Anne–Victorian Lapham-Patterson House, 626 North Dawson Street, was built in 1885 as one of the first winter "cottages" in Thomasville. The striking residence was equipped with its own gas-lighting system, hot and cold running water, and built-in closets. None of the ground-floor rooms is rectangular or square. Access to the upper floors is by a set of stairs around the dining room's rear-centered fireplace.

Several buildings on the grounds of the Thomas County Historical Society and Museum, 725 North Dawson Street, hold surprises for young and old. One surprise is the last original Victorian bowling alley still standing in Georgia, perhaps even in the South. Another is a display of fashionable party gowns from the period 1820–1940.

All Saints Episcopal Church, 443 South Hansell Street, was built about 1881. Jacqueline Kennedy attended mass here when she retreated to Thomasville following the assassination of President Kennedy.

It's not surprising that the kind of influence and money that existed almost 100 years ago assured a quantity and quality of cultural events. That legacy remains today at the Thomasville Cultural Center. Housed in a renovated 1915 school building at 600 East Washington Street, the regional center accommodates the visual and performing arts and also contains a genealogical and art reference library.

Thomasville is a Main Street USA community, where the historic architecture in a multiblock area of downtown has been preserved and renovated. Southern Destination—the 1915 train depot—has been renovated to award-winning status and boasts restaurants and specialty shops.

Although encompassing only two acres, Thomasville's Rose Test Garden, at 1842 Smith Avenue, features more than 250 species represented by 2,000 plants—some of which are for sale. The historic Rose City itself boasts more than 25,000 rosebushes and is the site of the annual Rose Show and Festival. Begun in 1921 and today one of the South's premier spring events, the festival is always the week preceding the fourth Friday in April. Events include a rose exhibit and competition, parade, theater productions, Miss Thomasville/ Georgia Rose Queen Pageant, Rose Patch Country Fair, and sports and culinary events.

Thomasville's most cherished landmark, The Big Oak, dates from 1685 and is enrolled in the National Live Oak Society. Its gargantuan branches cover an entire block and overhang two streets—Monroe and Crawford—on which the height of vehicles is restricted to protect the tree. Currently it has a 162-foot limb span, is 68 feet tall, and has a 24-foot trunk circumference.

Lieutenant Henry O. Flipper's grave, in the old cemetery on Madison Street, is the resting place of the Thomasville native who was the first Black graduate of West Point. The State Farmers Market is Georgia's second largest fresh produce market.

Four magnificent Victorian mansions house sumptuous bed and breakfasts: Evans House—an 1898 Victorian

Neoclassical house at 725 South Hansell Street; Our Cottage on the Park at 801 South Hansell Street; Grand Victoria Inn—an 1893 Victorian Eclectic house at 817 South Hansell Street; and 1884 Paxton House—a Victorian Gothic at 445 Remington Avenue. Deer Creek Bed and Breakfast is located in a contemporary house at 1304 South Dawson Street.

The most magnificent and accessible plantation in Georgia is Pebble Hill Plantation, south of town on US 319. The estate was established for growing cotton in the 1820s by Thomas Jefferson Johnson—a planter, politician, and founder of both Thomasville and Thomas County.

The present sprawling, extravagant, Georgian and Greek Revival mansion dates only from 1936. The original structure was built in 1827, replaced by a Neoclassical structure in 1850, then added onto several times. A 1901 addition created a loggia more than ninety feet long that was the only survivor of the devastating fire in 1934 when the central house burned. Fortunately, almost all the priceless possessions were saved.

Abram Garfield, an architect and son of President James A. Garfield, designed the present house as well as the elaborate gatehouses, a country store, and a dairy barn.

Here plantation life is defined: a self-sufficient realm that served as a place of solace for the privileged. Over the years formal gardens were created, and garages, guest houses, and service buildings were added as well as stables and kennels, a dispensary, dog hospital, fire engine house, family schoolhouse, tennis court, swimming pool, bathhouse, and cemetery. Be sure to allow yourself plenty of time to tour the grounds in addition to the house.

Pansy Ireland Poe, the last owner, accumulated vast art treasures. Today you can glimpse a bygone era of hounds and horses, carriages, and antique cars. Antiques—furnishings, porcelain, silver, crystal, and glassware—and fine art, such as thirty-three original Audubon paintings and hound paintings by European and American masters, coexist beside bronzes by western artist Hughlette "Tex" Wheeler and other objets d'art depicting sporting motifs. What began as a collection of arrowheads became a significant display of Indian memorabilia.

Special events throughout the year include the Candlelight Christmas Tour and a grand Plantation Ball during Thomasville's Rose Festival.

While you can only visit and dream at Pebble Hill, you can actually stay at nearby Susina Plantation Inn—a bed and breakfast that's about as close as you'll ever come to the Tara of your imagination. Susina is situated on the Meridian Road twelve miles south of Thomasville. Follow the signs off US 319. Keep an eagle eye out; the signs aren't easily seen.

This gracious Greek Revival home was built in 1841 by architect John Wind—who then built the 1850 version of Pebble Hill—and sits on 115 acres of lawns and woodlands, all that remain of the original 7,600 acres. Tremendous moss-shrouded oaks and magnificent magnolias shade the white-columned villa. Contemporary amenities include a lighted tennis court, swimming pool, stocked fishing pond, and jogging trails. In a departure from the usual bed and breakfast concept, Susina includes in the price a five-course dinner with wine. With prior reservations, you can have dinner without staying overnight.

Return to Thomasville and go east on US 84 to Quitman, which claims to have one of the largest turn-of-the-century historic districts in the nation. You can get a brochure for the historic driving tour at the Chamber of Commerce, 900 East Screven Street.

A few more miles east on US 84 will bring you to Valdosta—last stop on the Plantation Trace. Visit Valdosta's three historic districts and twenty-six other points of interest using the driving tour brochure from the convention and visitors

Thirteen columns, one for each colony, adorn the Crescent House in Valdosta

bureau at 1703 Norman Drive. The 1889 Crescent House, at 904 North Patterson Street, features a mirrored fireplace, ballroom, gold leaf-tiled bathroom, and a circular veranda supported by thirteen massive columns. The Chamber of Commerce is in the Ola Barber Pitman House, 416 North Ashley Street, home of the second manufacturer of Coca-Cola.

The Lowndes County Historical Society Museum, at 305 West Central Avenue, is a repository of records, old photographs, exhibits of naval and Sea Island cotton industries, and displays of Valdosta and Lowndes County history.

Paintings, sculpture, and other works of art, and local and traveling exhibits, are displayed at the Lowndes/Valdosta Cultural Arts Center, 1204 North Patterson Street.

Moody Air Force Base, ten miles north of town, is the home of the 347th Tactical Fighter Wing. Tours can be arranged in advance with the Public Affairs Office.

If you have not previously visited the Okefenokee Swamp, described in Coasting Along Georgia's Seaboard, you might want to do so. The west entrance is at Fargo, reached by heading east on State 94.

A jaunt through the Plantation Trace should slake your thirst for antebellum history and architecture and open your eyes to the natural wonders, sports possibilities, and man-made attractions just waiting for you to discover them. The easygoing lifestyle and extravagant homes and plantations, coupled with Indian history and plentiful opportunities for hunting and fishing, make the Plantation Trace the closest thing to the opulent Old South you'll find anywhere.

In the Area

Albany Local Welcome Center, 225 West Broad Street, Albany, GA 31701, 912-434-8700.

Bainbridge-Decatur County Chamber of Commerce, P.O. Box 736, Bainbridge, GA 31717, 912-246-4774.

Georgia Visitor Information Center, I-75, Lake Park, GA, 31636, 912-559-5828.

Moultrie-Colquitt County Chamber of Commerce, 329 North Main Street, Moultrie, GA 31768, 912-985-2131.

Quitman Chamber of Commerce, 900 East Screven Street, Quitman, GA 31643, 912-263-4841.

Thomasville-Thomas County Local Welcome Center, 109 South Broad Street, Thomasville, GA 317092, 912-225-5222.

Tift County Chamber of Commerce, P.O. Box 165, Tifton, GA 31793, 912-382-6200.

Tifton/Tift County Tourism Association, 100 North Central Avenue, Tifton, GA 31793, 912-386-0216.

Valdosta and Lowndes County Chamber of Commerce, 416 North Ashley Street, Valdosta, GA 31601, 912-247-8100.

Valdosta-Lowndes County Convention and Visitors Bureau, 1703 Norman Drive, Suite F, Valdosta, GA 31602, 912-245-0513.

12 ~

Antiques Trail and Other Treasures

Getting there: Take US 23 or State 20 to McDonough.

Highlights: *Antiques, vineyards, lakes and waterfalls, a Trappist monastery, antebellum and Victorian architecture, Claxton Fruitcakes, and the Rattlesnake Roundup.*

Georgia boasts several other trails: Antiques Trail, Miracle in the Mountains Loop Tour, Treasures Between the Trails, and the Wiregrass/301 Trail. Some are short enough to explore in a day or add to your investigation of another trail. Others cover a lot of territory but may not have numerous attractions. Some include towns and cities that are described in other chapters.

Antiques Trail

Like a bloodhound on the scent of its quarry, you'll be quivering with anticipation when you set out on the Antiques Trail.

Whatever type of antique strikes your fancy, you'll surely find it from among the 100 vendors, stretched over a nine-county, nine-city area south and east of Atlanta.

With the exception of Griffin, all the communities along the trail have been described at length in the chapters on the Antebellum Trail or the Peach Blossom Trail, or are covered in this chapter in the section on Treasures Between the Trails, so refer to them for information on historical sites and other attractions that you can enjoy while you're in the area.

The trail begins in McDonough, at US 23 and State 20, which boasts the largest, single-day antique market in Georgia. Several antique shops are scattered within walking distance of the beautiful courthouse square.

From McDonough, take State 20 southwest to US 19, then south to Griffin.

Griffin, a Georgia Main Street city located at US 41 and State 155, is in the heart of the Golden Triangle formed by Atlanta, Macon, and Columbus. While shopping for antiques, you can also tour thirty-eight sites in Griffin's historic district, dating from 1850 to the early 1900s, with a brochure from the Chamber of Commerce, at 1315 West Taylor Street, or from the Downtown Council/Main Street office, at 115 State Street. The Stonewall Cemetery is where more than 500 Confederate soldiers who died in the Battles of Atlanta and Jonesboro are buried. The southern-colonial 1859 Bailey-Thebault House, 633 Meriwether Street, serves as the headquarters of the Historical and Preservation Society.

Continue south of US 41 to Barnesville, at State 36 and US 41 (see the Peach Blossom Trail).

Take US 41 east until it meets I-75 at Forsyth, then go south on I-75 to Macon, an antique lover's heaven. Dreams are made of the antiques and collectibles you can find in the twenty-five shops and antique malls. Smiley's Macon Avenue

161

Antique Mall is located south of town on Hawkinsville Road. Downtown contains seven shops; the Ingleside/Vineville Avenue area boasts three. Wander through four more shops in the Forsyth Road/Bass Road/Riverside Drive area. Boling-broke sports another four shops (see the Antebellum Trail).

Continue south on I-75 to down-home Perry, where the Southeastern Antiques and Collectibles Market is held the fourth weekend of each month at the Agricenter (see the Peach Blossom Trail).

Return to Macon and go northeast on State 48 to Milledgeville, which offers antique shopping galore, as does Eatonton, where antebellum homes line the tree-bordered streets. Time seems suspended in Madison, north of Eatonton on US 441, where you can experience the Old South. The town is a treasure trove of historic structures as well as unique antique shops. All three towns are described in the Ante-bellum Trail.

From Madison, take either I-20 west, or the more scenic US 278 to Covington, whose quaint, magnolia-shaded historic square abounds with shops purveying antiques and other collectibles (see Treasures Between the Trails).

A journey through Central Georgia's Antiques Trail may be hard on the pocketbook but it's sure to be satisfying to the soul.

Miracle in the Mountains Loop Tour

This 170-mile Northwest Georgia trail includes some of the sites of both the Blue and Gray and Chieftans Trails as well as more attractions. Lookout Mountain is the home of Rock City Gardens, Ruby Falls, and the Incline Railway.

Take State 157, the Lookout Mountain Parkway, south to State 136, and turn west to Cloudland Canyon State Park, which has a series of waterfalls as well as hiking trails, camping, and cabins. From the park, return to State 157 and continue south to the town of Cloudland, where you might enjoy a reasonably priced steak dinner at The Lookout Restaurant or an overnight stay at the Victorian Parlor B&B.

Take State 48 to Summerville, noted for the murals painted on the sides of buildings in the business district. The Riegeldale Tavern, patterned after an English pub, is open daily.

North of town on US 27 is Paradise Gardens, a maze of abstract, symbolic sculptures and structures by visionary Howard Finster. Southeast of town on US 27 is James H. "Sloppy" Floyd State Park, a popular day-use park with outstanding fishing.

Continue on US 27/State 1 to Rome. Attractions at Berry College—the largest campus in the world—are the Martha Berry Museum and Art Gallery; Berry's home, Oakhill; a huge overshot waterwheel; the Gothic Ford Buildings; and more.

From Rome, take US 441 to Cave Spring, an antiques mecca. Lake Marvin has a wooded glen with a large spring and small streams, waterfalls, camping, fishing, hiking, and boat rental.

From Cave Spring, return to Rome via US 441, go north on State 53 to Calhoun, then take State 136C to Villanow—literally a country crossroads. Stop by the Villanow General Store, the oldest continuously operating general store in the region, at the intersection of State 136 and State 201.

Continue north on State 136 to State 193 to visit The Georgia Winery, which produces premium wines and champagnes using a secret freeze-fermentation method. The winery itself is on State 193 twelve miles south of St. Elmo in the valley of Lookout Mountain. The Taste Center and Outlet Store is on State 2 at exit 141 off I-75.

Continue north on State 193 to Chattanooga or turn east on State 2 to I-75. You have completed the Miracle in the Mountains Loop Tour.

Treasures Between the Trails

Nestled between the upper portions of the Antebellum and Peach Blossom Trails, this five-county area was first home to the Lower Creek Nation of Native Americans. It has produced two former governors and now country music star Trisha Yearwood. The region will get worldwide attention during the 1996 Centennial Olympic Summer Games, when the equestrian events take place here.

Begin the ninety-mile trail with Conyers, on I-20 east of Atlanta, which was once a train stop between Atlanta and Augusta. The Old Jail Museum in Historic Olde Town is one of the stops on the self-guided tour. Homes of early settlers and the Rock Store can be found in Cost Mill Park. The town's new 1,139-acre Georgia International Horse Park will host the 1996 Olympic equestrian events.

A unique place to visit is the Monastery of Our Lady the Holy Spirit, at 2625 State 212. The monastery was founded in 1944 by a group of Trappist monks who practice self-sufficiency. Their first plan was to cultivate all their own food, but they weren't very successful.

However, the monks do bake delicious honey-laced breads, which they sell in the Abbey Store along with books and products from other Trappist monasteries—creamed honey from Holy Trinity Abbey in Utah, jams from St. Joseph's Abbey in Massachusetts, and bourbon fudge and cheeses from Gethsemani Farms in Kentucky. The breads are only $1.50 a loaf, so buy several—one to munch on while you're on the road and some to freeze. The other food items are generally less than $5.00. Bonsai trees are available in the greenhouse.

Absorb the monastic-style peace in the lovely church or out on the grounds, lake, and gardens. Visitors are invited to join prayer services.

Continue east on I-20 to Covington at State 81. Get a brochure for a self-guided driving/walking tour of the well-preserved historic downtown district and neighborhoods of antebellum and Victorian homes. Notable landmarks include the 1850 Graham-Simms House, at 1155 Floyd Street, boyhood home of a Confederate general, and 1828 Swanscombe, at 1164 Floyd Street. Said to be the first clapboard house in town, it was the home of another Confederate general. Home tours are available with advance reservations.

Seventy soldiers who fell in the Battle of Atlanta are buried in the Confederate Cemetery. The First United Methodist Church, 1113 Conyers Street, was a hospital for both Confederate and Union wounded.

Known as "a gracious southern city of yesteryear," Covington stood in for six years as Sparta, Mississippi, in the CBS series *In the Heat of the Night*. On your tour, look for familiar landmarks from the series.

Fox Vineyards, on State 11, eight miles from the city, offers tours and wine tastings. For more information, call the Newton County Chamber.

From Fox Vineyards, proceed north on State 11 to Social Circle—so named because early residents gathered to socialize around the town well. Today, a replica of the original well symbolizes the friendliness and generosity that residents stand for. The Historic District includes more than fifty Victorian homes and shops built before 1900. Housed in a Greek Revival mansion, the Blue Willow Inn Restaurant, 294 North Cherokee Road, serves a sumptuous southern buffet. In addition to enjoying good food and southern hospitality, you can tour the premises and grounds.

Continue north on State 11 to Monroe. This enchanting town boasts nine historic districts listed on the National Register of Historic Places. Several homes have a significant historical interest in addition to their architectural beauty. The 1845 Davis-Edwards House has a mystery room featured in the children's book *Uncle Robert's Secret*, by Wylly Folk St. John. On McDaniel Street the homes of two former governors face each other.

Retrace State 11 south past I-20 to lovely Monticello, incorporated in 1808. It is the home of country music star Trisha Yearwood. The gracious buildings around the Town

Be sure to bring home some sweet, tasty Vidalia onions

Square were constructed between 1889 and 1906. You can get a walking tour brochure from the Monticello-Jasper County Chamber of Commerce.

Outside of town, the 11,500-acre Oconee National Forest contains two wildlife refuges, camping, a recreational area on Lake Sinclair, and two boat access areas on Lake Oconee.

Go west on State 16 to Jackson, where you will complete Treasures Between the Trails. The great outdoors abounds around Jackson. First check out the town's history at the Butts County Historical Society, 431 College Street. Then head south to High Falls State Park, located on the Piedmont fall line. The park is the site of Georgia's southernmost waterfall, a 650-acre lake, camping, and water sports. The Dauset Trails Nature Center, 1,000 acres on Mt. Vernon Road off State 42, provides six miles of hiking trails, as well as plant identification and ecology programs. Indian Springs State Park is also nearby. Jackson Lake, north of town, has 4,700 acres, a 135-mile shoreline, and all water sports.

Wiregrass/301 Trail

The wiregrass region is in the southeastern part of Georgia about twenty-five miles inland from the coast. It is named for the tough, wiry grass native to the area. For many years US 301, completed in the 1940s, was the major route from New York to Florida along the Eastern coast. US 301 runs 165 miles north-south in Georgia, traversing the eastern parts of the Colonial Coast and Magnolia Midlands regions. This scenic trail is profuse with stately pines, moss-covered oaks, and unspoiled rivers. It travels through small southern towns full of history as well as unique shops and restaurants. Roadside stands sell Georgia specialties such as Vidalia onions.

We'll begin our tour at the southern end of the trail at Folkston, one of the entrances to the primeval Okefenokee Swamp. The town and the swamp are described in Coasting Along Georgia's Seaboard.

Take US 301 north to Jesup. Downtown, on Broad Street, is the Little Red Caboose and Railroad Section House, the Wayne County Historical Society's museum of early 1800s memorabilia. The huge steeple clock on the 1903 Courthouse, on Brunswick Street, continues to chime out the hour. The Carter House, at 311 South Wayne Street, is an exceptional example of Queen Anne Victorian architecture. You can pre-arrange tours at I.T.T. Rayonier, the world's largest chemical cellulose-producing pulp mill in the world. The Trowell House, 256 East Cherry Street, is a bed and breakfast and restaurant located in a captivating Queen Anne Victorian mansion. Numerous water sports are available on the Altamaha River, Lake Lindsay Grace, and Cherokee Lake.

About six miles out of town on US 301 is the site of the December 13-17, 1864, Civil War clash known as the Doctortown Railroad Trestle Battle. This was one of the last battles before Sherman's federal troops marched on Savannah.

The next stop as you proceed north on US 301 is Glennville, where you can tour Bland Farms—a major producer of Vidalia onions. For those not familiar with these tasty onions, they are world-famous for their sweet flavor and crisp texture. Because of a unique combination of soil and climate, Vidalia onions grow only within a small area of South Georgia. Although we've never tried it, many aficionados claim that Vidalia onions are so sweet, you can eat one raw like an apple. Naturally you can buy onions in season as well as cookbooks with onion recipes and storage tips.

Farther north on US 301 is Claxton, home of the Claxton Fruitcake Company. In all our lives, we've never met anyone who would admit to liking fruitcake. The sweet, heavy cakes are often the subject of ridicule by late-night talk-show hosts, but someone must like them. The downtown bakery ships more than 6 million pounds annually. You can tour the bakery and get a free sample during the baking season, September through mid-December. Also downtown is the 1923 Evans County Courthouse, an exceptional example of Neoclassical design.

Claxton may be famous for one thing even above its fruit-cakes—its annual March Rattlesnake Roundup.

Four miles west of town on US 280, you can tour a bee-keeping operation at Wilbanks Apiaries—a honey-producing and pollination facility. You'll want to bring home some honey—maybe to go along with the bread you bought at The Monastery of Our Lady the Holy Spirit in Conyers (see Treasures Between the Trails).

Head north again on US 301, take I-16 west, and take a short detour to Metter, on State 46. First explore the restored 1930 lumber mill Commissary at the Metter Local Welcome Center and Chamber of Commerce, at exit 23 on State 121 and I-16.

Metter is the home of religious broadcaster Michael A. Guido. His complex on State 121/North Lewis Street includes The Sower Studios, which is the radio and film center, and Guido Gardens, among which are a gazebo, fountain, and prayer chapel.

Several churches in the area are historically signifi-cant. Old Lake Church, five miles east of town on State 46, is one of the oldest Primitive Baptist churches in the state, founded in 1823. The present structure was built in 1839. Across the street is one of the largest country cemeteries in the state. Salem Church, built in 1879, retains hand-hewn boards.

A rare shrub called Elliottia grows at the Charles C. Harrold Nature Preserve, which is also home to the gopher tortoise—a rare and endangered species and Georgia's only native tortoise.

Return to US 301 and head north to the last stop on the trail—Georgia's 301 Trail Headquarters in Statesboro, where you can experience what residents call "sincerely southern hospitality."

Home of Georgia Southern University, the fastest-growing university in the nation, Statesboro offers the GSU Museum filled with changing exhibits and hands-on displays. However, the pièce de résistance is a dinosaur skeleton. The university offers year-round symphony and theater performances. Also on campus is the Herty Nature Trail in the Herty Memorial Pine Forest.

The Statesboro Historical Tour and Downtown Statesboro Architectural Walking Tour feature historic homes, grounds, and prominent landmarks. You can get brochures from the Boro Bungalow, which is Statesboro's Welcome Center and gift shop, at 204 South Main Street.

Some highlights of the tour include the revitalized Main Street district and the Savannah Avenue Historic District—Statesboro's first suburb, developed in the early 1900s. The Magnolia Garden, located on a restored turn-of-the-century farm, features ten acres of rare and native plants.

At the Welcome Center you can make arrangements to tour Braswell Foods and Sunny South Pecans, two local industries that package food favorites.

Statesboro has a lovely bed and breakfast and restaurant at the historic Statesboro Inn, 106 South Main Street. The Beaver House, 121 South Main Street, is a boardinghouse restaurant—all you can eat, family style—located in a Neo-classical Revival mansion.

These trails are only suggestions of ways to explore Georgia's bounties. The best trail in the state may be the one you make up yourself.

In the Area
Antiques Trail

Griffin-Spalding County Chamber of Commerce, 1315 West Taylor Street, Griffin, GA 30223, 404-228-8200.

Main Street/Downtown Council Office, 115 State Street, Griffin, GA 30223, 404-228-5356.

Miracle in the Mountains Loop Tour

Chattooga County Chamber of Commerce, 4 College Street, Summerville, GA 30747, 706-857-4033.

Dade Development Corporation, Box 849, Trenton, GA 30752, 706-657-7513.

LaFayette Area Chamber of Commerce, 304 North Main Street, LaFayette, GA 30728, 706-638-1930.

Rome Tourist and Convention Committee, P.O. Box 5823, Rome, GA 30161, 706-295-5576.

Treasure Between the Trails

Butts County Chamber of Commerce, 143 East College Street, Jackson, GA 30233, 404-775-4839.

Newton County Chamber of Commerce, 2100 Washington Street, Covington, GA 30209, 404-787-3868.

Monticello-Jasper County Chamber of Commerce, 115 East Green Street, Monticello, GA 31064, 706-468-8994.

Wiregrass/301 Trail

Claxton/Evans County Chamber of Commerce and Welcome
Center, US 301 North, Claxton, GA 30417,
912-739-2281.

Glennville Local Welcome Center, 134 South Main Street,
Glennville, GA 30427, 912-654-2000.

Wayne County Tourism Board, 124 N.W. Broad Street,
Jesup, GA 31545, 912-427-2028.

Statesboro Convention and Visitors Bureau, 204 South Main
Street, Statesboro, GA 30458, 912-489-1869.

800-LOVE-301 for a brochure on attractions, lodging,
restaurants, fairs, and festivals.

Magnolia Midlands Travel Association, P.O. Box 729,
Eastman, GA 31023, 912-374-6383.

Index

Index

Seminole State Park,
Bainbridge, 68, 150
Skidaway Island State Park,
113
Stephen C. Foster State
Park, Fargo,108
Sweetwater Creek State
Park, Lithia Springs, 45
Tallulah Gorge Park, Toccoa,
130
Terrora Park, 130
Unicoi State Park, 134
Veterans Memorial State
Park, Cordele, 7–8
Wildlife preserve, Lake
Oconee, Eatonton, 18
Willis Park, Bainbridge,
149
PEOPLE
Carter, Miss Lillian, 7
Carter, President Jimmy, 7,
47
Davis, Jefferson, 33, 50,
93–94
Grant, Gen. Ulysses S., 31,
39
Harris, Joel Chandler, 16
Jackson, Gen. Stonewall,
50
Lee, Gen. Robert E., 50
Mitchell, Margaret, 49
Oglethorpe, Gen. James,
101, 113, 115
Roosevelt, President
Franklin D., 60
Sherman, Gen. William
Tecumseh, 31, 39, 40, 41,
43, 48–49, 100, 136
Talmadge, Eugene, 87
Talmadge, Herman Eugene,
87

Tubman, Harriet, 12
Walker, Alice, 16
REENACTMENTS
Atlanta History Museum,
Atlanta, 49
Battle of Reseca, Reseca, 35
Battle of Rome, Rome,
35–36
Tunnel Hill, 34
REFUGES
Blackbeard Island, 114
Wolf Island, 114
RESORTS (*See also* HOTELS,
INNS, and BED AND
BREAKFASTS)
Callaway Gardens, Pine
Mountain, 57–59
The Cloister, Sea Island,
117
Dillard Resort, 132
Forrest Hills Mountain
Hideaway, Dahlonega,
124–125
King and Prince Resort, St.
Simons Island, 117
Sea Palms, St. Simons
Island, 117
Sky Valley Resort, Dillard,
132
Tate House, 80
Villagio di Montagna,
Cleveland, 125

SCENIC DRIVES
Dahlonega's Magic
Mountain Trail, 125
North Georgia mountains,
81
Richard Russell Scenic
Highway, North Georgia,
122

STORES and MARKETS
  Abbey Store, Monastery of
    Our Lady the Holy Spirit,
    Conyers, 164
  Babyland General Hospital,
    Cleveland, 125
  Barnesville Hardware,
    Barnesville, 139
  Easterlin Country Store,
    Andersonville, 4
  Four Winds Indian Museum
    and Trading Post, Tiger,
    130
  History Store, Dahlonega,
    124
  Nut House in the Grove,
    Hawkinsville, 87
  Old Sautee General Store,
    Sautee, 127
  Pecan Store, Fort Valley, 141
  Rock Store, Conyers, 164
  State Farmers Market,
    Thomasville, 154
  Stuckey's Candy, Eastman,
    87
  Tara Relics, Jonesboro, 137
  Towanda's, Juliette, 144
  Villanow General Store,
    Villanow, 163

TOURS
  Black history driving tour,
    Columbus, 63
  Bland Farms, Glennville,
    168
  Blue Bird (Bus) Body
    Company, Fort Valley, 141
  Braswell Foods, Statesboro,
    170
  Chickamauga/Chattanooga
    National Military Park, 30

Claxton Fruitcake Company,
  Claxton, 169
Columbus Ledger-Enquirer,
  Columbus, 63
Consolidated Mines,
  Dahlonega, 124
Dolley Madison, Columbus,
  63
Garden Tour, Perry, 142
I.T.T. Rayonier, Jesup, 168
Jekyll Island Club Historic
  Landmark District tram
  tour, 118
Kinnett Dairies, Columbus,
  63
Lane (Peach) Packing
  Company, Fort Valley, 140
Moody Air Force Base,
  Valdosta, 158
Negro Heritage Trail,
  Savannah, 99
Paddle wheeler cruises,
  Savannah, 98
Pebble Hill Plantation,
  Thomasville, 155
Princess Augusta paddle
  wheeler, Augusta, 90
Sapelo Island Estuarine
  Research Reserve, 114
Sunny South Pecans,
  Statesboro, 170
Sunshine Biscuits,
  Columbus, 63
Swift Textiles, Columbus,
  63
Tom's Foods, Columbus, 63
Trebor Plantation,
  Andersonville, 6
Trolley, Milledgeville, 15
Vidalia onion farms and
  plants, 88

Index

Titles in the Country Roads series:

Country Roads of Connecticut and Rhode Island
Country Roads of Florida
Country Roads of Georgia
Country Roads of Hawaii
Country Roads of Idaho
Country Roads of Illinois, third edition
Country Roads of Indiana
Country Roads of Iowa
Country Roads of Kentucky
Country Roads of Maine
Country Roads of the Maritimes
Country Roads of Maryland and Delaware
Country Roads of Massachusetts, second edition
Country Roads of Michigan, second edition
Country Roads of Minnesota
Country Roads of Missouri
Country Roads of New Jersey
Country Roads of New Hampshire, second edition
Country Roads of New York
Country Days In New York City
Country Roads of North Carolina
Country Roads of Ohio
Country Roads of Ontario
Country Roads of Oregon
Country Roads of Pennsylvania
Country Roads of Southern California
Country Roads of Tennessee
Country Roads of Texas
Country Roads of Vermont
Country Roads of Virginia
Country Roads of Washington

All books are $9.95 at bookstores.
Or order directly from the publisher (add $3.00 shipping and handling for direct orders):

Country Roads Press
P.O. Box 286
Castine, Maine 04421
Toll-free phone number: **800-729-9179**